Actors' Handbook
2013-2014

a pro directory

© Casting Call Pro 2013

New edition published 2013 by

Casting Call Pro
131/132 Upper Street
Islington
London N1 1QP

www.castingcallpro.com

A CIP catalogue record for this book is available from the British Library

ISBN 978-0-9556273-4-7

Set in Frutiger & Serifa
Designed and produced by Prepare to Publish Ltd
(www.preparetopublish.com)

Printed in Britain by
Polestar Wheatons, Exeter

Contents

Acknowledgements

We are very grateful to the following individuals, companies and organisations for their contributions to this book. Their insight and advice is invaluable for rising and aspiring actors. Many thanks are due to:

Cameron Baird

Phil Barley, TheatreDigsBooker.com

Helen Bennedict

Douglas Brown, Robert Harper & Rosie Thorpe

James Bollanack, The Voiceover Gallery

Richard C.Burke & Rachel Roberts, Industry Hollywood

Ione Butler

Tim Dawkins, Quantum Theatre

Pamela Hall, Actors' Creative Team

Ben Humphrey, Worcester Rep

Kassam Jaffer, Longcord Training and Consultancy

Forbes KB

Sonia Kaur and Alexandar Fodor, Actor's One Stop Shop

Brian Parsonage Kelly, Brood Management

Dayo Koleosho, Nick Llewellyn & Sarah Hughes, Access All Areas

Miss L, Professionally Resting

Anthony Meindl, Anthony Meindl's Actor Workshop

Benjamin Newsome

Tim O'Donoghue

Mike Parkes, TWD Accountants

Adam Rood, AlreadyLabelled.com

Lindsay Rule, Drama UK

Rachel Strange, Brighton Fringe

Cathy Thomas & Amelia Forsbrook, IdeasTap

Elliot Travers, Actor Coaching for Drama School
Philip Weaver, East 15 Acting School
Michael Wharley, Michael Wharley Photography
Zoë Wanamaker

And lastly, a big thank you to the Casting Call Pro members who kindly shared their experience, talent and advice. If you're interested in finding out more about anyone featured in the book simply search their name on Casting Call Pro.

If you have any questions about this book or feel an organisation or company ought to be included in future editions please send details to **info@blue-compass.com**.

Foreword

 castingcall**pro**

© Noel Light-Hilary

If you're reading this book, chances are you're already an actor or you are seriously considering a career in acting. Either way there is a journey ahead of you, and it's likely to be one of the most rewarding, frustrating, challenging, humbling and edifying journeys you will ever undertake. Few professions offer such highs and lows, from the rigours of training, the struggle to find work and the pressures of auditioning, through to the incredible, inimitable rush of performing.

Actors' Handbook is brought to you by Casting Call Pro, one of the leading resources for professional UK actors. Casting Call Pro was built for actors to share knowledge and advice and we have taken the same approach with this book, allowing those in the industry to contribute to its contents. Actors' Handbook really is your essential guide to getting work and getting noticed.

I hope you enjoy it!

Phil Large – CEO
Casting Call Pro

Introduction

Professionally Resting

Small-time actress, big-time rester

THIS INTRODUCTION WAS KINDLY WRITTEN BY UK ACTOR AND BLOGGER, PROFESSIONALLY RESTING

Been in anything I might've seen? Got any exciting roles coming up? Why don't you just get a part in EastEnders? However long you've been acting for, I can guarantee that you've had at least one of those questions launched at you. And you won't be asked when you do have exciting acting work coming up or have just finished something hugely exciting that you want to tell the world about. No. You'll be fielding these questions when the only thing in your diary is when you really ought to be giving your pyjamas a wash.

So why on earth do we put ourselves through it? Despite how social acting seems on the surface, it's a surprisingly solitary job and you spend a lot of your time wondering where you've gone wrong. Surely you can't be the only one who has caught themselves actually shouting at a computer screen when every casting call out there is for something you are not. It can't just be you that has found themselves in a church hall in the middle of nowhere pretending to be a frantic moth who's on the run from horse-riding aliens. And please say someone else has found themselves sat under an anglepoise lamp in a director's basement, nervously humming 'Happy Birthday.' Please. Of course you're not alone. Ask any actor about what it's really like when you dedicate your life to putting on a funny voice and donning a moth-eaten, dubious disease ridden hat and they will all have at least one horror story that will tug furiously on your cringe muscles.

Acting is a demanding friend. It needs constant reassurance from us and regularly requests eye-watering levels of financial and emotional support. New headshots, updated showreels, ridiculous amounts spent on travel. And after all that, we're lucky if we get to hang out with it while on a schools tour or an unpaid film where most of our time together is spent nibbling on rapidly decaying sandwiches. Deep down we know that acting would probably prefer to be spending its time with others but do we give up? Do we heck. Instead, to try and keep acting interested, we engage in 'resting'; the most inappropriately named activity that ever was. To keep our flaky mate in the manor to which it is accustomed, we land ourselves in sprawling call centres, dingy classrooms and rainy high streets handing out soggy leaflets on a Wednesday morning.

So there must be something that keeps us here despite family members asking when we're going to get ourselves a proper job or friends having to constantly bail us out. Someone recently commented on my blog and asked why I don't give up trying to be an actor. They commented anonymously but it was clear that they weren't an actor because, if they were, then they'd know why. It's the little skip that makes its way into our step after a particularly good audition. It's getting that call and dancing around the house in your pyjamas when you find out you got that job. It's nailing that line you've been agonizing over for weeks. It's finally wrapping at 2am on a freezing cold riverbank with only a flimsy summer dress protecting your modesty. It's that realisation that maybe, just maybe, you did well to not listen to the careers advisor.

Despite its pitfalls, ask any actor and they'll defend their work till the pantomime cows come home. Yes, we complain about it. Yes, we find ourselves constantly wishing it was a bit more fair. And yes, we may sometimes look on in envy while our friends get to go on lovely holidays and live in houses where mice don't outnumber people. But, in spite of all these things, I think we all count ourselves very lucky to be doing the best job in the world.

Miss L blogs about the trials and tribulations of being an actor at **www.professionallyresting.blogspot.co.uk** *and you can follow her at* **@ProResting** *on Twitter.*

"Despite its pitfalls, ask any actor and they'll defend their work till the pantomime cows come home"

Chapter 1
Training

Drama School Q&A

Q. Do I need to go to Drama School?

© Piotr Kowalik

'Many of the things you learn at drama school can't be learned just by getting up and having a go at acting; raw talent is one thing, good technique to sustain a whole career is another. I thought I was a pretty good actor until I trained, only then did I realise how far I had to go, and still do. It's hard to grow as a performer and get rid of bad habits without proper professional guidance and important to spend a concentrated amount of time honing your essential acting tools (physical, vocal, intellectual and emotional). You also get the opportunity to really stretch yourself and learn from your mistakes in a safe working environment. It would be great if all young actors could join a top acting company straight out of school or university and learn everything they needed from watching and working alongside the leading actors, but that doesn't happen. You need a reputable drama school to launch you into the business – that school's name is a seal of quality attached to the 'product' you want to sell: yourself. It's almost the only way to get seen by the better agents who can move your career forward and support you when you are starting out. It's worth pointing out that given the cost and time involved, choosing the right drama school for you is absolutely essential. Research all the schools, visit them if you can, and find out which schools are producing the actors who are getting the kind of work you want to do. Settling for a second rate training is the worst start you can have: bad training means bad career prospects.'
Dominic Brewer

© Rosie Still

'The drama school I attended instilled in me a confidence that I wouldn't have had otherwise. It provided me with a safe environment to practise various methods and to discover what worked for me and what didn't. Because it's always a very honest place to be, you get to learn a lot about yourself which helps when applying for roles.'
Christopher Keddie

Training at a reputable drama school is perhaps the best route into professional acting. Not only does it afford you a thorough grounding in acting and an opportunity to hone your craft with like-minded people who share your drive and passion whilst demonstrating your ongoing commitment to your calling, it also gives you credibility in the eyes of casting professionals. As long as the school you attend is reputable and you demonstrate a willingness to learn, you'll be better placed at the end of the course to succeed as an actor – with a greater understanding of your craft, hands-on acting experience under your belt and a graduation showcase which agents commonly attend. But be warned – places at good drama schools are very over-subscribed and the application and audition process is highly competitive.

Most age requirements will generally stipulate that you have to be 18 years of age or over. If you're too young to be eligible for a three year drama school course, the traditional route is stage school. Most of these are private and therefore there will be considerable fees to meet, although there may be scholarship options. Another option is to attend youth theatre groups or drama workshops. Check out The National Association of Youth Theatres (**www.nayt.org.uk**) and The National Youth Theatre (**www.nyt.org.uk**) for more information (National Asssociation of Youth Drama **www.youthdrama.ie** and Scottish Youth Theatre **www.scottishyouththeatre.org** in Ireland and Scotland respectively).

Q. How do I choose a course?

There are lots of factors you should take into consideration when choosing your school. Your checklist:

- Start by looking at the institution itself: is it a university or college dedicated to drama, media or stagecraft?
- How long has it been established and how long has it been offering a drama course?
- What are the facilities like?
- Who would be teaching you – do the teachers have the necessary experience to teach you what you need to know to succeed?
- Do they put on an end of year showcase? If so, how well-attended is

it in terms of agencies and what's their track record of students finding representation?

- Check out the institution's past record by researching the alumni – what do past students go on to do?
- Location is important - you may be spending up to three years there, so you have to like the place! If you'd have to move away from home remember to factor in living costs: university digs, food, bills etc all add up on top of tuition fees.
- How much are the course fees? Remember that financial help and support is out there in the form of Student Loans and scholarships.
- Course selection is pivotal – do you want a broad cross-section of acting disciplines or to focus on stage or screen acting, for example? The school's website will give you a good idea of the course content, but you can always contact them directly should you have further questions - they'll be happy to help with your enquiries.

You might also want to consult Drama UK, which is the national body championing quality drama training in the UK. In addition to the guide opposite, do check out their website, where a great section on funding your training can be found.

About Drama UK

THIS GUIDE WAS KINDLY WRITTEN BY DRAMA UK

Drama UK was formed in 2012 following the merger of the Conference of Drama Schools (CDS) and the National Council for Drama Training (NCDT).

Drama UK continues to fulfil the functions of both NCDT and CDS. This includes championing quality drama training in the UK through advocacy, assurance and advice and providing a unique link between the theatre, media and broadcast industries and drama training providers in the UK.

The organisation gives a united, public voice to this sector; encourages the industry and training providers to continue to work together; offers help and advice to drama students of all ages; and awards a quality kite mark to the very best drama training available.

Drama UK's mission is three-fold:
1. **Advocacy** – to lobby the Government and key influencers so that they understand the importance of high quality drama training to the UK's economy and society.
2. **Advice** – to provide anyone interested in drama and the careers related to it with a route map to the training and opportunities available whatever their age or ambitions.
3. **Assurance** – to ensure that drama training in the UK is of the highest standard through a rigorous programme of quality assurance.

Drama UK Quality Assurance
Drama UK now delivers the Quality Assurance role originally undertaken by NCDT.

Training

The main quality mark it awards is Accreditation, and this is only available to vocational, conservatoire style training, i.e. full-time, practical training with contact hours of at least 30 hours a week, designed to equip students with the necessary skills to enter the profession. These courses are run by Drama UK Member schools.

Drama UK Accreditation exists to give students confidence that the training they choose is accepted by the drama profession as being relevant to the purposes of their employment; and that the profession has confidence that the people they employ who have completed this training have the skills and attributes required for the continuing health of the industry.

Accreditation is monitored regularly by top members of the broadcasting, theatre and media profession.

Drama UK is currently reviewing its quality assurance function. For the latest information on Accreditation and for details of a new quality mark called Recognition, please visit the Drama UK website **www.dramauk.co.uk**

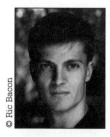

© Ric Bacon

'When applying I looked at specific acting courses accredited by Drama UK and visited the open days, as well as looking through the previous graduates and what they had gone on to do.'
Edward Charlton
www.edward-charlton.com

© Paul Aitchenson

'I went for well-known schools with good ratings on the Guardian website, and schools that I could afford using the student loans scheme.'
Andrew Silverwood
www.about.me/andysilverwood

© Mark. A. Davis

'I wanted somewhere that would offer me mainly practical training, and allow me to experience many different styles and genres of theatre and TV/Film acting. I got that when I trained at Northampton - it allowed me to realise what I was best at!'
Lauren Backler
www.laurenbackler.co.uk

Q. What's the application process like?

The first stage will involve applying to the school directly. A standard application form will ask for basic details, your acting experience so far and the reasons for wanting to attend the course. Check the applications deadlines as these will vary from course to course and school to school, but getting your application in sooner rather than later is always advisable. There should be no fees for applying but you should bear in mind that if you're called for audition the school will usually charge an audition fee in addition to your own travel and accommodation expenses to attend.

The audition process will also vary from school to school - most likely a mixture of monologues, group work, improv, movement, workshops and interviews. Depending on the course you may also have to prepare a song and/or dance.

Be prepared – competition for places will be extremely high.

Advice to Drama School Auditionees

THIS GUIDE WAS KINDLY WRITTEN BY PHILIP WEAVER, HEAD OF BA ACTING AT EAST 15 ACTING SCHOOL

Preparation

- Research the course that you are applying for – all this information is available in the prospectus / online. Come and see a third year public production (free tickets can be arranged if you book in advance).
- When selecting monologues try and stay within your own casting age / range and make sure you have read the whole play that the speech comes from.
- Make sure the monologues are contrasting – show different character choices. (Monologues you select can often reveal as much about your own personality as they do about the character).
- Do not over rehearse the monologues, stay open-minded about them. However, learn the lines very thoroughly – remembering lines should be the last thing on your mind when in an audition.
- Prepare at least one speech in your own accent.
- Prepare at least one reserve monologue, Shakespeare/Jacobean or modern.

On the day

- Be yourself.
- You should be well-rested and prepared to work for up to 7 hours, including presentation of your audition pieces and workshops in which you may be redirected in them (the ability to respond to direction and instruction quickly and concisely is essential for an actor).
- Don't panic if you forget your lines, keep your focus, take a breath, go back one line and pick up where you left off (This is far more impressive than asking to start again).

- In group work and improvisation be open to other people's ideas and willing to contribute your own.
- Be prepared to sight read a difficult piece of prose – practise is the only real preparation for this. If you are dyslexic, as many professional actors are, tell the panel member/s in advance and you will be given extra time to prepare.
- Be able to discuss a professional theatre production that you have seen recently.
- Try and enjoy yourself, the more relaxed you are the more likely you are to succeed.

What are we looking for?

Our objective is to ensure that you, and we, get the most out of the day and that you have the opportunity to show yourself at your best.

Trainability: we are not looking for fully formed actors ready to walk onto a West-End stage. We are looking for energy, dedication, spontaneity and potential. Our training prioritises the 'ensemble spirit'; you must demonstrate suitability for this kind of work.

Be prepared to discuss why you want to act and why you want to train at East 15 Acting School.

One of the UK's most innovative acting schools, East 15 has been providing professional training for those wishing to work in theatre, film, TV, radio and related fields for almost 50 years.
www.east15.ac.uk

© Grant Appleton

'Workshop, audition and interview – this involved the exploration of physical ability and work with text. I researched the nature of the course and prepared and rehearsed a monologue. The interview gave me the opportunity to express my passion for what I want to achieve and explore in my career.'
Siobhán McKiernan

© Patrick Clarke

'*ALRA auditions for both of its sites at once in an all day audition process. Monologues in front of all auditionees in the morning and a workshop and interview in the afternoon. They are very friendly and welcoming and always give feedback on the day so you can improve. It would be a good choice for your first audition if you are doing the rounds.*'

Kate Benfield

© Martin Richardson

'*The audition process for the Birmingham School of Acting required students to complete an online application. Once selected, you would then meet with two tutors for a 20 minute audition slot in which you then performed two contrasting monologues – one classical, one from within the last 20 years. You would then have a brief interview and were asked questions about your interests and motivations, as well as your reasons for selecting the school and what other schools you had applied to. If you are recalled (usually you can wait up to 3 weeks to hear of the outcome) you are then invited back to the school for a full days workshop and audition with around 40 other people. You are given a number and divided into two groups.*

For me, the morning part of the session involved a group movement, dance and improvisation workshop followed by a song performed in front of the Head of the Singing department. The afternoon then consisted of a group audition where you were required to perform both monologues in front of a panel of tutors. This took around 2 and a half hours. This entire process took around 5 months: choosing monologues, songs, rehearsing, applying and auditioning, up until receiving the letter to say I had gained a place. The process of auditioning, performing in groups and being recalled is a standard format for all major drama schools and required a great deal of research into each school, reading more plays than I've ever read in my life and more travelling round the country in a year then I ever want to do again. It is horrifically hard work, a once in a lifetime experience and well worth it once you gain a place.'

Evelyn Campbell

Actor Coaching for Drama School

THIS GUIDE WAS KINDLY WRITTEN BY ELLIOT TRAVERS, ACTOR AND ACTING COACH AT ACTOR COACHING FOR DRAMA SCHOOL

These days gaining a place at drama school is more competitive than ever. It is therefore important to go into the audition as well prepared as possible. But if the key to success is preparation, how do you prepare?

First and foremost, find the right monologues. Without these you really will come unstuck. Choosing the right monologue can often seem intimidating, but it is important to find the joy in this process as later in your career you will spend a lot of time scrawling through different scripts! When searching it is important to make sure you keep to the spec. If they ask for a contemporary monologue after 1980, you must find a contemporary monologue after 1980. There are a lot of playwrights out there and each one has their own individual writing style. Read plays by a variety of different playwrights and pick out the ones whose writing style you can easily understand and to whom you feel a strong attachment. You should be drawn in by the semantics, rhythm, context and subtext of the writing.

Once you have chosen the playwrights that speak to you, you then need to read each of their plays in order to find a character you feel a connection to, as being connected to both your character and the text is something that drama school assessors will look out for in an audition. 'Being connected' means having a true understanding of the situation your character is faced with and understand exactly why they've reacted the way they have. Your character should have as many similarities to you as possible. Selecting a character that is more similar to yourself will make your performance more truthful. It will

21

"The trick is to expect the unexpected and not to be surprised by what they ask – you need to have the confidence that you can carry out the task in hand"

also give you less character development work to do that you might not otherwise be comfortable doing at this stage in your acting career.

When finding a monologue, save yourself time and effort by flicking through the play before you read it to make sure there is a suitable monologue in the book to start off with - the expected length will be stated in the audition brief. When you look at the character's monologue it is important to make sure the monologue has an appropriate 'arc' in it. 'Arc' means a line of action, ie, it should have twists of thoughts in the character's mind as well as a climax and some form of conclusion at the end.

Once you've chosen a monologue you then have the task of putting it on its feet and bringing it to life - and don't forget you will most likely need to have variety of monologues on hand to show the panel your range.

Preparing monologues is a vital part of the audition process, but it is only half of the practice. Every drama school audition is different; some may call you in purely to do a monologue, others may do a workshop day focusing on your voice, others may look at your imagination and movement. The trick is to expect the unexpected and not to be surprised by what they ask – you need to have the confidence that you can carry out the task in hand.

Drama School, not to mention the acting industry as a whole, is a high-pressured environment and assessors not only want to know that you can act under pressure, they want to see that you can act well under pressure. To see how well you cope they'll be looking at a vast number of different elements including your confidence, ability to take direction, creativity, clarity, decision making, improvisation and adaptability.

This may all seem daunting but don't fear, there is help available: talk to the professionals! People specialise in coaching you every step of the way to bring out your best skills as an actor, from working with you to find and prepare your monologues, to advising you on the realities of the industry, the standard you're at and the standard you need to get to in order to gain a place at drama school. After all, these are the people that have experienced this process firsthand and who know all about what it's like to be an actor - who better to help you make your first steps in the industry successful ones.

Not sure where to find a coach? Contact Actor Coaching for Drama School to find the best tutor for you. They will be able to give you advice over the telephone and give you a free consultation. www.actorcoachingfordramaschool.co.uk

Q. What can I expect from the course?

Hard work! You'll be expected to attend classes, rehearse and study day after day. A full-time acting course is rigorous and extremely demanding, emotionally and physically. Do not embark upon a full-time drama course unless you are prepared for the challenge of an-encompassing lifestyle that demands self-discipline and commitment.

Your course will likely include modules on different theories of acting, physical exercises, voice work, movement classes, roleplays, scene work and full productions. Check the school's website for more information about specific course components.

© RB Headshots

'Stressful, intense, exciting, draining - depending on the project. They definitely put you in situations that are foreign to you as much as they can, which mean you have to tackle your blindspots or weaknesses head-on so you knew that when it's hard it's going to be worth it.'
Katerina Elliott

© John Nichols

'Hard! In a lot of the time. 9-9 sometimes if in a production. Also intense. I didn't understand that word before but it's constant. You rehearse with people, go out with them, drink with them, then learn lines, research, act. But if you love acting you will love it all.'
Sarah Eve

© Robin Savage

'Tough, long hours, constant homework and the stress of finding your niche hanging over your head, but the atmosphere was that of a family and everyone was always willing to get stuck in and help you out if times got too rough.'
Chris Keyna
www.chriskeyna.com

Q. Should I enroll in a foundation course?

Some schools and a growing number of organisations offer foundation or 'taster' courses. These courses can be short-term, part-time or intensive one year and are designed to give you an introduction to acting. It can help to have completed a foundation course before applying to drama school, but they shouldn't be viewed as a substitute for a full-time drama course. You should also be wary of courses promising too much for a short investment of your time and a large investment of your money. As with all other courses, check the credibility of the institution, course, teachers and facilities before parting with any cash.

Q. What about mature students?

As with any degree-level course, you can expect a large proportion of the other students to be in their late teens or early twenties – but that doesn't mean there aren't openings for mature students. Schools are generally very receptive to older applicants. Many people decide to retrain or have a career shift, and the older actor may be in a better position to finance their training. Do check with the drama school first however, as some do have upper age limits. Even if they don't, steel yourself for being thrown into the society of people younger than yourself. If you can't find a suitable full-time course, a part-time one may be worth considering – though these are less likely to lead to as many career opportunities.

It's Never Too Late

THIS GUIDE WAS KINDLY WRITTEN BY HELEN BENNEDICT

© David Price

Much as I loathe the label 'mature' student, I recognise it's what other people consider me to be as I was 44 when I went to East 15. No doubt any study later in life is a big step, but a Masters in Acting comes with its own special challenges and, of course, rewards. No matter your motivation for going, you are unlikely to be there because your family or teachers or friends expect or demand it. In fact, when you announce that you are heading to drama school, those people, in my experience, fall into two camps – the ones who are insanely jealous that you're following your dream and those that just think you are insane.

Everyone's journey will be different, but these are a few of the aspects that I discovered during mine.

Before the course

The audition process: I'm not going to lie to you, it takes some bravery to walk into an audition room, full of (predominantly) twenty somethings, to deliver your 4 minutes of life-changing text. Particularly when many of the twenty somethings have come straight from drama degrees. Despite doing lots of research, I simply didn't have the knowledge or experience to truly understand what the audition process was going to be like. Not to mention struggling to find 'age appropriate' monologues.

My first surprise was just how different all the auditions were. I had decided I was giving this one shot (no year after year applying for me), so I applied for nine schools and received auditions from all of them. They had all asked for between one and three 1-2 minute monologues; one Shakespeare/Jacobean, one contemporary. The interpretation of what contemporary was varied wildly from 20th/21st Century through to post 1956 or post 1986, which meant I prepared about 10 different pieces, as call-backs where you couldn't use the same material also had to be factored in. I worked on this process alone and it was tough.

As I made my way through my auditions, I discovered that I personally fared best in the places that invested some time and found out about the whole me, not just my ability to deliver two monologues and leave. The schools that included improvisations, sight-reading, games, scene direction, interviews and movement seemed to prove much more successful (and enjoyable) than the 'give your Shakespeare, give us your contemporary, thank you, you can leave'. It also provided me a stronger sense of what the school would be like. Whilst I wanted to be chosen, I also wanted to choose.

Once you get in and before you start
Now it's real. Practical considerations include where you're going to live, how your family/friends will cope with your time commitments (see below) and financial implications. These have to be worked out at any age, there are just usually more layers at this age.

When you start
The really big factor is TIME. A Masters in Acting is all-encompassing. Unlike many research based Masters programmes, drama school is very high contact and in addition to the hours that you're physically at school, you'll be researching, reading, preparing, doing assignments and working on projects. There won't be much of you left to share around outside of your drama school world. You will need supportive family and friends who embrace your journey with you. They may feel excluded from the intense experiences you have with your peer-group and jealous of the relationships you develop. It's hard to explain the experiences you have and the relationships you develop at drama school.

"In acting training I was encouraged to play, try, experiment, feel, be brave, follow my twin, find the joy, be curious and non judgemental"

27

The biggest learning curve for me was, having come from a corporate and business background, just how ingrained 'getting things right' was. In business we tend to be rewarded for being careful, using analysis, data, justification, judgement, being able to cover your bases and demonstrate proof. In acting training I was encouraged to play, try, experiment, feel, be brave, follow my twin, find the joy, be curious and non judgemental. It was a LONG time since that kind of behaviour had been encouraged and I found over-thinking a hard habit to break. A long-standing old demon such as 'I can't sing', which was one I'd held onto for approximately 35 years (thanks to some insensitive school teachers), also had to be overcome. And yet, to pass my course, I had to find my voice and it turns out I can sing just fine – what a pity I missed out on 35 years of enjoyment.

Fitness and stamina is important. Actor training is physically and emotionally demanding. No matter your age, you will need to be able to move, dance, headstand, cartwheel, flip and roll. You'll also need to put in long hours and show up on time the next day. Embrace it, love it and show those twenty somethings how it's done!!

The key advantage of training at this age, I believe, is that we've already learned how to get out of bed, do a full days work, wedge in the rest of our life, budget, grow a thick skin and bounce back from adversity.

After qualifying

So, the good news is that 'I am doing well', post qualifying. I place that in quotation marks, because it is what everyone tells me, not necessarily how I feel. I have an agent, I'm being seen for castings, sometimes by the same Casting Director on more than one occasion, I have done paid work. But I won't lie, it's a tough path. At my age I have LOTS of very experienced competition, women who have been doing this a long time, with infinitely more credits than me.

What works in my favour is that I'm a new face and I believe that is helping. It also helps that I have an 'every woman' face. That, is pure luck! The lack of interesting roles for women, the stereotyping, the jobs that really require a model not an actor – all frustrate me no end!

How you juggle working as an actor with the rest of your life will depend on what the rest of your life looks like. You will need to be 'on call' and super flexible for castings if you want any work at all. So think about how you will structure the other work you do around acting if you need to earn an income. It needs to be something that can be dropped at short notice.

In the end, choosing to go to drama school later is, I believe, rarely about wanting to be discovered or becoming famous. It is about pursuing a passion and making sure you don't end up on your death bed with the 'I wish' regrets of not having tried.

Many thanks to Helen for sharing her experience, advice and insight with us. Her website is **www.helenbennedict.weebly.com**

Q. How about training for actors with disabilities?

There's a growing demand for actors from a broader and more inclusive spectrum of society. Check the main drama schools and find out what their policy is, and what their facilities are like in terms of accessibility and the provision of hearing loops in rehearsal spaces, for example.

Check out out Chapter Four for a guide by Access All Areas, a theatre company for people with learning disabilities based in Hackney, London. Access All Areas recently joined together with the Central School of Speech and Drama to work on an exciting new training opportunity for actors with learning disabilities. You can visit their website at **www.access-all-areas-uk.org**.

You might also find Disability Arts Online **www.disabilityartsonline.org.uk**, Graeae Theatre Company **www.graeae.org** and Mind The Gap **www.mind-the-gap.org.uk** useful resources.

Q. Any final tips?

© Pete Millson

'Apply for an accredited course at a drama school as this does give you advantages in the business. I believe you can follow any other specialist courses later but it is harder to get into the accredited courses so it is worth putting that as a priority early on.'
Alison Williams-Bailey

© Martin Richardson

'Work hard at your monologues, finding unique ones that are appropriate to you and the criteria; perform them to people outside of your bedroom. Research the schools and don't apply somewhere that you don't think you'd want to go to, and know why you want to go to each school. Realise the size of the competition and don't take it personally. If they offer advice, take on board everything they say. Have fun and be a joy to work with.'
Pippa Caddick

© Rory Flint

'Don't choose a school because of its reputation alone. It is no guarantee of work. Choose a school which will suit what you want to achieve and be prepared to work very hard, before and after you leave.'
Ross Mcnamara

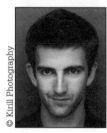

© Kirill Photography

'Do your research on the schools. Not every school is right for everyone. Also don't be disheartened if you don't get in first year. Most 18 year olds aren't well enough prepared for a 3 year course. Many don't get through first time round but with additional training and experience get it the next time.'
James Ackroyd-Smith
www.jamesackroydsmith.wix.com/actor

Funding Your Training: Useful Links

STUDENT LOANS
The Student Loans Company
www.slc.co.uk
Student Finance Wales
www.studentfinancewales.co.uk
Student Awards Agency for Scotland
www.saas.gov.uk
Student Finance Northern Ireland
www.studentfinanceni.couk

SCHOLARSHIPS & BURSARIES
Scholarship Search
www.scholarship-search.org.uk
BBC Performing Arts Fund
www.bbc.co.uk/performingartsfund
Dance and Drama Awards
www.gov.uk/dance-drama-awards
Student Cash Point
www.studentcashpoint.co.uk

HELP, GUIDANCE & SUPPORT
Direct Gov – Student Finance
www.gov.uk/student-finance/overview
Direct Gov – Professional and Career Development Loans
www.gov.uk/career-development-loans/overview
Money Saving Expert
www.moneysavingexpert.com/students
Drama UK
www.dramauk.co.uk/funding
Prospects
www.prospects.ac.uk/money.htm
NUS – Money and Funding
www.nus.org.uk/en/advice/money-and-funding

The Other View: My Non-Traditional Route into Professional Acting

THIS GUIDE WAS KINDLY WRITTEN FOR US BY FORBES KB

© Alex Claus at Lexart.co.uk

Hey guys! My name is Forbes KB. Who the heck are you I hear you say? Well I market myself as a 'trucking actor' because, as well as being a freelance truck driver, I'm also now a jobbing actor and have appeared in 4 episodes of the HBO mega-series Game of Thrones, the feature film Harry Brown alongside Sir Michael Caine and Made of Honour alongside Patrick Dempsey, as well as a raft of other well known productions you will have watched on your telly boxes in addition to hundreds of other productions you won't ever have seen or heard of. In 2012 I appeared as a credited actor in 7 feature film releases and this year I've got 5 ... so far.

I became a professional actor in June 2004 after ending a 19 year career in the aviation industry.

All the way through my teenage years and early twenties theatre, specifically musical theatre and light opera, was my passion. It soon became clear when my aviation career started to take off that shift work and fixed rehearsal schedules were always going to clash so I walked away from acting to follow the aviation path. Aviation took me all over the world initially, in the commercial airline environment working at Inverness Airport and London Gatwick, moving into private and VIP aviation based in Dubai and then onto selling and marketing the IT solutions that support the aviation industry based out of Rome, Milan and the company's head office in Geneva.

The offer to take voluntary redundancy in late 2003 gave me the perfect opportunity to return to acting but this time, instead of amateur dramatic and local operatic societies, I made the decision to go professional. Had I known at that time how hard it was going to be to actually make a living from the world of acting, I may have made a different choice but I've never been a quitter so here I am nearly 9 years later and I'm still here, still making films and still paying my bills. It's fair to say that in 2004, having not done any acting at all for the best part of 20 years, I didn't have a clue, and with a wife and three children to support taking 3-5 years off to go to Drama School simply wasn't an option, so I set out a business plan which was designed to take me from zero experience to a credited role in a Hollywood feature film within 3 years. If I didn't get that Hollywood feature film credit by June 2007 it was back to the drawing board, so the clock was ticking. Now don't get me wrong! The ambition was not to become a celebrity or a star, I could have gone down the reality TV route if that was my intention. The goal was, and still is, to make a living and to provide for my family doing what I love to do and that is acting.

The business plan was broken down into major goals at the end of each year with milestones every three months along the way. For example, the goal at the end of year 1 was to secure an agent to help me open the doors to the Casting Directors. To get an agent I had to show them I could act so for the first 3 months I did nothing but background work to learn what a 1st, 2nd & 3rd AD actually did while earning at the same time. Terms like gaffer, best boy, key grip etc were all alien terminology to a complete novice like me, so instead of sleeping on the dining bus I spoke to everyone, watched everything going on around me and took notes. I was probably really annoying looking back at it but I learned so much in a very short space of time.

For the next 6 months, alongside the background work, I travelled all over the UK doing student films from Wales to Bournemouth, from Leeds to York, from Edinburgh to Bristol – anywhere there were

"I set out a business plan which was designed to take me from zero experience to a credited role in a Hollywood feature film within 3 years"

student filmmakers who needed actors I was there! I rapidly amassed over 40 short film credits during that period playing everything from a psychotic Russian mobster and a homophobic representation of God, to an alcoholic wife beating misogynist; I needed the footage to make a showreel with which I would attract my first proper agent and by April 2005 I had that first showreel! Looking back at it now is slightly embarrassing as rough doesn't even come close to describing that first ever reel, but it did the trick and I signed with my first agent. They got fired within a few months and my second agent didn't last much longer. In January 2006 I finally found an agent that was as ambitious as I was and who understood me better, and I'm still with them.

Doing background work or being a Supporting Artist has never been viewed favourably as a career path in the UK by cast or crew alike, even though over in the US it's seen as a rite of passage that every screen actor has to go through, so I probably wouldn't recommend that route these days in the UK. That side of the business has changed considerably over the past few years and, in line with my business plan, I stopped doing SA work years ago. That being said, I still get the occasional call from the agencies to fill in here and there even though I'm no longer with them.

I suppose the moral of my story is that there are many ways to skin a cat and if you're determined, ambitious, act like a professional and treat everyone with respect you can be a professional actor with or without going down the traditional Drama School route.

So what advice would I give to anyone looking at a career in the world of acting?

Treat everyone with respect. Not everyone is as they may appear! The girl taking names at the door of an audition suite may well be the final decision maker. I found that out the hard way right back at the start of my journey and I was reminded of this encounter only recently! Some people have long memories and this is a very fickle business, so be polite and respectful to everyone on the way up, and I mean everyone! You never know who might be in position to help you in the future if you find yourself on the way back down again.

Get yourself known to everyone. Marketing yourself correctly is crucial! You may be the best actor on the planet but if the gatekeepers of our industry don't know you are out there how are you going to get cast in anything? That being said, bombarding the Hubbards or Nina Gold's office with hundreds of unsolicited emails, CV and headshots is not going to get you known for the right reasons. Do your research on what's in pre-production and who's casting what. Set up targeted campaigns and time your approaches carefully. Sometimes sitting back and just leaving it for a week or two can work wonders.

Talk to other actors. I recently set up the British Actors Network (**www.facebook.com/groups/BritishActors.Net/**) to help newcomers network with the old timers like myself. Experience is something no one can teach you at any drama school and you can learn a lot by just talking to your peers. The British Actors Network is a free networking group and we run free live networking events all over the country to bring actors at all levels together. I've been cast in a few decent feature film roles purely from contacts I would never have met other than through BAN so I can't emphasise strongly enough the power of networking! It can be a really lonely and insular profession if you're not as busy as you'd like to be and, let's be honest, for most of us jobbing actors that's most of the time.

Have an alternative source of income. That's where my trucking comes in. When I first started I knew I wouldn't make money from acting straight away so I got myself an HGV licence. As long as there are supermarkets that need stock and boxes with 'smiles on the side' there will always be trucking work. Theatre tours all have to move the sets around by truck and you'll never be on a film set that isn't surrounded by trucks, so it was an obvious choice for me. I also got 8 days filming on Casino Royale (2006) purely from being in the right place at the right time and moving a few 3-ways for the locations company. I was shooting a student short for Coventry University and tracked down the Bond people on location in Prague! We all have a steady stream of bills to pay and a less than steady income at best from our chosen profession. Having a flexible and reliable source of income outside acting is critical. If you've had a quiet month and the rent is due you'll

"There are many ways to skin a cat and if you're determined, ambitious, act like a professional and treat everyone with respect you can be a professional actor"

walk into the audition room NEEDING the job as opposed to WANTING the job and that's a recipe for disaster! That desperation will come through in your audition performance and will be your ultimate downfall.

Be proactive and keep on top of it. Don't just sit there waiting for your agent to call because 9 times out of 10 they probably won't. If the opportunities aren't happening for you and all your acting friends are being seen for all sorts of stuff there's usually a reason. There could be something about your headshots, your showreel or your CV. Don't be afraid to ask for a peer review or a career assessment from another industry professional - there are a hundred different reasons why the casting directors may not be kicking down your door and it may be blatantly obvious to someone else! Also if opportunities are thin on the ground, why not create your own work and get writing! Spielberg started making films in his parents' back garden with his school friends! No one is going to spoon feed you a successful acting career! Only you can make it happen and it takes years of hard graft to become an overnight sensation.

Keep learning every chance you get. Do workshops, classes and courses to improve your skills! Get your driving licence, your motorbike licence, learn to ride a horse, learn to fence, take a martial art, tap dancing, singing lessons ... just keep learning ... anything that ticks another box on your CV! If Pacino, Theron and Berry (Halle not Nick) still take regular classes, which they do, so can we! It's a massively over-populated industry and opportunities in the current climate are sparse. Giving yourself an additional skill may make all the difference at that key casting.

Expert advice: My Non-Traditional Route into Professional Acting

At the end of the day guys we're here because we love to perform, to create characters, to transport our audiences into other worlds and other times. We love the adrenalin hit just before the curtain goes up on a first night performance or just before the director says action at the start of our big dialogue scene. Our audiences laugh with and at us, cry with us, shout and scream at us and sympathise with the situations our characters find themselves in. We are the storytellers, the Hans Christian Andersons of our time and the world would be a much poorer place without us, so don't you ever let anyone tell you to get a real job ... acting is a real job! It's as real as it gets!

The British Actors Network is a free social networking site for anyone involved in the British acting scene at any and all levels: **www.facebook.com/groups/BritishActors.Net.** *Forbes' personal website is* **www.forbeskb.british-actor.net**

After Drama School: Why On-Going Acting Training is Essential

THIS GUIDE WAS KINDLY WRITTEN BY ANTHONY MEINDL

'Skill is only developed by hours and hours and hours of beating on your craft. I've never viewed myself as particularly talented. Where I excel is ridiculous, sickening work ethic.' – Will Smith

We've all heard variations of 'it takes 10,000 hours of practice to become great' and that Michael Jordan got cut from his high school team then practiced every single day until the next year's tryouts and then made the team (he could also fly, so that helped!).

We all know it takes hard work to become great at anything. Duh. Acting is no exception. In fact, on-going acting training can inform all aspects of a student's life.

Internally the acting student will go deeper and deeper into their craft, accessing parts of their personality that are unique and specific. These things are often buried under years of 'trying to fit in'. But they are the traits that make us special and interesting to watch onstage and onscreen. Good teachers will act as guide for the student (the answers are within, young grasshopper).

On-going training should push actors to explore all aspects of themselves – the good, the bad, the ugly (cue spaghetti western soundtrack) – all of it. This process of self-discovery sharpens the actor's ability to experience emotions truthfully during a performance. And it's what makes actors riveting to watch.

No two actors will interpret a scene the same way. With training, actors become more present, more aware of who they are and their own unique perspective on the world.

"No two actors will interpret a scene the same way. With training actors become more present, more aware of who they are and their own unique perspective on the world"

Acting classes are also a fantastic way to make connections with other artists, create projects together, get seen by casting directors, and network. A supportive community of fellow actors can be essential during those rough first few years of trying to make it as an actor in Los Angeles or New York or London or wherever. It helps to have that foundation and know that other actors are going through the same struggles and triumphs ('I booked the job!') as you are.

Find a teacher that inspires you to grow as a human being. And practise, practise, practise.

Anthony Meindl is an award-winning writer, director, producer, and Artistic Director of Anthony Meindl's Actor Workshop (AMAW) in London: www.anthonymeindl.com/actor-school-london.htm. Follow Meindl on Twitter @AnthonyMeindl.

A-Z of Drama Schools & Colleges

There are so many many institutions offering acting training across the UK that it's really worth taking the time to do your research and find the course that's best for you.

To help you make a start, we've made a list of the most commonly attended institutions by Casting Call Pro members – and included testimonials about their time there. The following is by no means an exhaustive list and there is more information on course providers at **www.castingcallpro.com/uk/college.php**.

In these listings we have focused on Undergraduate and Postgraduate courses, but do keep in mind that many of these institutions also run a wide variety of short courses, Diplomas and Foundation-level programmes - you can find out more via their websites.

We've also included the number of CCP members who have attended these institutions. These figures are correct at the time of going to press.

ACADEMY OF LIVE & RECORDED ARTS
STUDIO 24
THE ROYAL VICTORIA PATRIOTIC BUILDING
JOHN ARCHER WAY,
LONDON SW18 3SX
WWW.ALRA.CO.UK
CCP MEMBERS: 628
COURSES:
BA (HONS) ACTING
MA ACTING
ALRA aims to equip actors and theatre technicians with those skills fundamental to a productive and creative life in the performance industries. ALRA is dedicated to helping students of all backgrounds and ages to enter the world of live and recorded arts. ALRA has a distinguished record of producing professionals prepared and ready to work.

'The deciding factor for me in going to ALRA was the real family atmosphere within the school. There are so few students at any one time that you tend to know everyone. That was important for me – I felt at home there, and still feel part of the community a year after graduating. The training doesn't specialise in one technique or medium, they simply throw ideas at you for three years and see what sticks. Everyone that left from my year left with their own techniques and style and, in my opinion, everyone an individual and a better actor.'
Tom Skitt

'15 months of life-changing, intensive actor training which concluded with showcases in both Manchester and London.'
James Verity

ARTS EDUCATIONAL SCHOOL LONDON

14 Bath Road
Chiswick
London W4 1LY
WWW.ARTSED.CO.UK
CCP MEMBERS: 1205
UNDERGRADUATE COURSES:
PART TIME CONVERSION COURSE / B.A. Hons PERFORMANCE STUDIES
BA (Hons) Acting for Film & Television
BA (Hons) Musical theatre
POSTGRADUATE COURSES:
MA Acting
MA Screenwriting
MA Musical Theatre Creative Practice
Our ambition is to provide the best quality training in musical theatre and acting for film and television in the UK.

'Arts Ed has trained me to such a standard that, even though I am just entering this business, I feel confident and excited to take on any project! It is also a lovely environment, encouraging everyone as individuals, and nurturing you in the way you need to get the best out of you. I am so glad I went there because of its screen acting training. I have been on a professional set since graduating and I understood everything and didn't feel intimidated in the least – an invaluable feeling as a beginner.'
Tamaryn Payne

BIRMINGHAM SCHOOL OF ACTING

Millennium Point
Curzon Street
Birmingham B4 7XG
WWW.BCU.AC.UK/PME/SCHOOL-OF-ACTING
CCP MEMBERS: 753
COURSES:
BA (Hons) Acting

BA (Hons) Applied Performance (Community and Education)
MA Acting
MA Acting: The British Tradition
MA Professional Voice Practice
Birmingham School of Acting (BSA) is an exciting, contemporary place to train for your professional drama career in the theatre, community, film or TV. Our state-of-the-art studios in Birmingham's Millennium Point are second to none, and the school buzzes with creativity.

'Quite possibly the best three years of my life! I learnt a huge amount about acting, the industry and life in general. I would recommend it to anyone looking to start an acting career.'
Tim Thurston

'Intense and very rewarding, great teaching and a supportive atmosphere.'
Lee Garrett

ROYAL CENTRAL SCHOOL OF SPEECH AND DRAMA

Embassy Theatre
Eton Avenue
London NW3 3HY
WWW.CSSD.AC.UK
CCP MEMBERS: 1609
COURSES:
BA (Hons) Acting
BA (Hons) Drama, Applied Theatre and Education
BA (Hons) Theatre Practice
MA Acting
MA Acting for Screen
MA Movement Studies
MA Music Theatre
MA Theatre Studies
MA/MFA Voice Studies
Central's mission is to place students at the centre of its work. Central develops practi-

tioners and researchers who shape the future of theatre and performance across the UK and beyond.

'I have learnt a huge amount from the Post Graduate Musical Theatre course. It was a very good use of my time and funds. Teachers are very helpful and passionate. I highly recommend it!'
Candy Ma

'The only course of its kind in the UK, I was continually impressed by the breadth of actor training we were exposed to, plus the commitment and knowledge of both the in-house tutors and visiting lecturers.'
Tiana Harper
www.tianaharper.com

DRAMA CENTRE LONDON
CENTRAL SAINTS MARTINS COLLEGE
GRANARY BUILDING
1 GRANARY SQUARE
KING'S CROSS
LONDON N1C 4AA
WWW.CSM.ARTS.AC.UK/DRAMA
CCP MEMBERS: 536
COURSES:
BA (HONS) ACTING
MA ACTING
MA SCREEN ACTING
Drama Centre London offers its students a unique blend of training methods. As part of Central Saint Martins College of Arts and Design and the University of the Arts London, Drama Centre provides an international outlook, a central London location and excellent learning and performance facilities.

'So far the best decision I made.'
Janina Blohm-Sievers

'Fabulous training. One of the best times of my life. Such fantastic mentors and the chance to work on the world's greatest plays, non-stop for three years.'
Dorothy Lawrence

DRAMA STUDIO LONDON
GRANGE COURT
1 GRANGE ROAD, EALING
LONDON W5 5QN
WWW.DRAMASTUDIOLONDON.CO.UK
CCP MEMBERS: 771
COURSES:
PG DIP 1 YEAR ACTING
PG DIP 2 YEAR ACTING
Drama Studio London was founded over 45 years ago. The original courses were designed to give the aspiring actor the best grounding in skills and approach in order to prepare for a professional career. That has remained our ethos.

'This course allowed me to grow as both an actor and a person. They have a very individual approach and know how to get the best from each student. I can't thank the tutors and my fellow students enough for the fantastic time I had!'
Corran Royle

'The year spent at DSL proved to be a significant foundation to the ongoing training I have had since graduation through professional work. You feel fully prepared and confident knowing you have undergone such an comprehensive and fundamental training programme such as Drama Studio London. The board of teachers and industry professionals at DSL provide a great opportunity to create strong networks within the industry as well as up to date knowledge and experience on the industry as well.'
Drew Elston

EAST 15 ACTING SCHOOL

HATFIELD
RECTORY LANE
LOUGHTON IG10 3RY
WWW.EAST15.AC.UK
CCP MEMBERS: 1684
COURSES:
BA ACTING
BA ACTING AND CONTEMPORARY THEATRE
BA ACTING AND COMMUNITY THEATRE
BA ACTING AND STAGE COMBAT
BA PHYSICAL THEATRE
BA WORLD PERFORMANCE
MA IN ACTING
MA/MFA IN ACTING (INTERNATIONAL)

One of the UK's most innovative acting schools, East 15 has been training actors, directors, producers and theatre technicians for stage, TV, film and radio for 50 years. East 15 offers a range of undergraduate and post-graduate courses, as well as summer courses, at campuses in Loughton and Southend.

'East 15 has provided me with a life changing experience both as a person and as an actor. I entered the course unsure of myself and unsure of the processes I should be using for specific roles and mediums of drama. However having now completed the course I feel confident in myself to enter auditions and leave having successfully secured the role.'
Elliot Travers

'I truly believe that East 15 Acting School was the best place I could have gone to. It changed my life - and that is no exaggeration. I was on the Acting and Contemporary Theatre course and although it was highly challenging and sometimes left me feeling, 'what am I doing here', I wouldn't have had it any other way. We had such variety in our training – physical theatre, devising, physical comedy and clowning, site-specific theatre, film and mixed media, writing workshops with April De Angelis, acrobatics… the list goes on. So I left feeling like a well-rounded performer – and a fearless one, able to do whatever was asked of me in an audition and more than capable of creating my own work without having to rely on anyone else to get it for me.'
Susan Lay

GUILDFORD SCHOOL OF ACTING

STAG HILL CAMPUS
GUILDFORD
SURREY GU2 7XH
WWW.CONSERVATOIRE.ORG
CCP MEMBERS: 920
COURSES:
BA (HONS) ACTING
BA (HONS) MUSICAL THEATRE
MA ACTING
MA MUSICAL THEATRE

Our mission is to enable our students and staff to work at the forefront of their profession. From our inception in 1935 we have been dedicated to high-level training for the performing arts, a close relationship between traditional and cutting-edge practices, and a vision of the value of integration across the art.

'Before joining GSA I did a summer school there and immediately I knew this is where I belonged, call it a feeling. Once I joined I was welcomed in with open arms and became part of the GSA family. GSA is warm and friendly and very supportive. I am very lucky to have studied there. Thank you GSA.'
Andrea Nodroum
**www.castingcallpro.com/uk/andrea
lorena.nodroum**

'This course has provided me with everything I need in order to start my career as a professional actor and I know I can always ask when I need support. It's been great!'
Joanna Leese

GUILDHALL SCHOOL OF MUSIC AND DRAMA

SILK STREET
BARBICAN
LONDON EC2Y 8DT
WWW.GSMD.AC.UK
CCP MEMBERS: 371
BA (HONS) ACTING
MA (HONS) ACTING

The Guildhall School is a lively, friendly community of actors, theatre technicians and musicians; the Drama Department itself is intimate and supportive. Our programmes are highly regarded in the acting profession for the thoroughness of their audition processes, the passion, quality and rigour of the teaching, the emphasis on the integration of craft training, the care and attention for the individual development of each student and the strong ensemble ethic shared by our staff and students.

'Would recommend this to anyone! Worth every penny.'
Jamie Trotter
www.jamietrotter.co.uk

'Guildhall is an excellent, accredited drama school with a very well established reputation. Although I was there many years ago, it still stands out as a centre of excellence.'
Tessa Wood

ITALIA CONTI ACADEMY OF THEATRE ARTS LTD

ITALIA CONTI HOUSE
23 GOSWELL ROAD
LONDON EC1M 7AJ
WWW.ITALIACONTI.COM/
CCP MEMBERS: 807
COURSES:
BA (HONS) ACTING

Italia Conti Academy is a world-renowned centre for actor training. It is one of the country's leading vocational acting courses with an emphasis on professional development and employability. We believe that acting is not just an art form but also a craft and our students leave the course equipped with the skills necessary to take up meaningful roles within the profession. The course is designed to encourage self-awareness as a 'creative entrepreneur' and our students are characterised by their imagination, flexibility and determination.

'I had the time of my life at Conti's, I changed so much in the space of 3 years, not just in my skills as a performer but as a person. I learnt new things that will stay with me for life. Conti's allows you to be who you want to be, and doesn't try to clone you into what they think the industry wants.'
Auriol Hatcher

'I thoroughly enjoyed my time at Italia Conti. They allowed me to realise where my strengths are and helped them to grow.'
Victoria Bilton

LONDON ACADEMY OF MUSIC AND DRAMATIC ARTS

155 Talgarth Road
London W14 9DA
WWW.LAMDA.ORG.UK
CCP MEMBERS: 1159
COURSES:
BA (Hons) Acting
MA Acting for Classical Theatre

LAMDA is an independent drama school, dedicated to the vocational training of actors, stage managers and technicians, directors and designers in the skills and levels of creativity necessary to meet the highest demands and best opportunities in theatre, film, radio and TV.

'Excellent training. It has left me with a toolbox full of skills which I can apply to the varied acting jobs on offer. Really wonderful teachers, I'd recommend it to anyone.'
Erin Hunter
www.erinhunter.co.uk

'My year at LAMDA was a life changing experience. I am thrilled to now be able to hit the stage with the support of such a fantastic school behind me.'
Audrey Rumsby

MANCHESTER SCHOOL OF THEATRE

Manchester Metropolitan University
Mabel Tylecote Building
Cavendish Street
Manchester M15 6BG
WWW.THEATRE.MMU.AC.UK
CCP MEMBERS: 377
COURSES:
BA (Hons) Acting

The Manchester School of Theatre at the Manchester Metropolitan University has a long standing international reputation for preparing students for careers as professional actors. Our graduates have found careers in all of the major theatre, film and TV companies including the BBC, ITV, the Royal National Theatre, the Royal Shakespeare Company as well as all of the major touring and regional repertory companies.

'I would have no hesitation in recommending Manchester School of Theatre as a place of study to any budding actor. The course offers such a wide and varied set of skills to be learned, staff who are so committed to the training and development of actors, and opportunities in the North West to rival any London School.'
Neil Gregor

'The best three years of my life. Wouldn't be the actress I am today without it.'
Christine Clare

MOUNTVIEW ACADEMY OF THEATRE ARTS

Clarendon Road
London N22 6XF
WWW.MOUNTVIEW.ORG.UK
CCP MEMBERS: 1482
COURSES:
BA (Hons) Performance (Acting)
BA (Hons) Performance (Musical Theatre)
MA/PG Dip Performance (Acting)
MA/PG Dip Performance (Musical Theatre)

Mountview offers the highest quality training for actors, musical theatre performers and directors. Our range of undergraduate and postgraduate courses instil all students with the skills required by the contemporary theatre, film, radio and TV industries. The courses are delivered in a highly supportive environment by staff who are experts in their field and who aim to produce actors and directors with the potential to be regularly employed in a varied industry. During training students will continually come into contact with numerous practitioners, all keen to pass on their wealth of experience, knowledge and advice.

'I owe so much to the wonderful people at Mountview. The amount of time they have for you, and the dedication they have to their work, is without parallel. The techniques that they employ have created such a massive difference to me in such a short space of time. Nor does the school simply train you before sending you off into the big, wide world; they remain with you, always offering support, advice, and even use of facilities.I couldn't recommend them more highly, and have only the most heartfelt thanks for all their work.'
Christopher Laishley

'Mountview was amazing for me - and I had auditioned for other courses and schools. Mountview allowed you to try everything and then take what you need to help you strengthen your skills.'
Philippa Burt

OXFORD SCHOOL OF DRAMA

SANSOMES FARM STUDIOS
WOODSTOCK OX20 1ER
WWW.OXFORDDRAMA.AC.UK
CCP MEMBERS: 404
COURSES:
DIPLOMA IN ACTING (3 YEARS & 1 YEAR)
The Oxford School of Drama is the youngest of the accredited drama schools. We have achieved phenomenal success in our short 26–year history and continue to dedicate ourselves to vocational training for actors.

'A very impressive course: challenging, real, honest, with a focus on collaborative, inventive work. Excellent tutoring in physicality and voice.'
Christine Wood

'Extremely intense and hard work, but well worth it in the end. I would highly recommend The Oxford School of Drama to anyone who is serious about entering the profession.'
Karlina Grace

ROSE BRUFORD COLLEGE

LAMORBEY PARK CAMPUS
BURNT OAK LANE
SIDCUP
KENT DA15 9DF
WWW.BRUFORD.AC.UK
CCP MEMBERS: 883
COURSES:
BA (HONS) ACTING
BA (HONS) ACTOR MUSICIANSHIP
BA (HONS) AMERICAN THEATRE ARTS
BA (HONS) EUROPEAN THEATRE ARTS
The School of Performance offers different approaches to training, leading to a range of specialised careers, roles and vocations. A healthy respect for tradition and craft is combined with innovation, contemporary work and an emphasis on new writing to allow you to experience and achieve a richness and diversity of performance. The School's international profile allows students to participate in stimulating cross-cultural exchanges, further enabling us to inspire, excite and train you as a creative artist who can use reflective practice and research as tools to become an independent thinker and a fulfilled, contributing professional.

'Rose Bruford is a fantastic and exciting school to learn and develop as an actor. Widely recognised as one of the leading drama schools in the UK under the influence of its president Sir Richard Eyre, it provides a broad, diverse and realistic grounding for the actor. In particular, Tony James gave excellent

tuition throughout the course, sharing his wealth of experience to us and advising us in all matters of the industry.'
James Lorcan

'An intensive acting course which creates intelligent and well-rounded practitioners with a variety of skills.'
Roisin Brehony

ROYAL ACADEMY OF DRAMATIC ARTS (RADA)

62-64 GOWER STREET
LONDON WC1E 6ED
WWW.RADA.ORG
CCP MEMBERS: 749
COURSES:
BA (HONS) ACTING
MA THEATRE LAB

RADA was established in 1904 and has built an outstanding reputation as a world-renowned centre of excellence, offering the best possible facilities, exceptional teaching and strong links with the industries that employ our graduates. RADA's student population is a diverse community, united by a shared passion for theatre-making. The Academy prides itself both on the professional standard of its student productions, which are attended by agents, casting directors and theatre practitioners, and on their track-record of employment in theatre, film and television.

'An extremely comprehensive course, both challenging and intensive.'
TJ Brett

'Very rewarding, intensive course in acting. Invaluable introduction to the profession.'
Grace Lyons Hudson

ROYAL CONSERVATOIRE OF SCOTLAND (FORMERLY RSAMD)

100 RENFREW STREET
GLASGOW G2 3DB
WWW.RCS.AC.UK
CCP MEMBERS: 409
COURSES:
BA ACTING
BA CONTEMPORARY PERFORMANCE PRACTICE
BA MUSICAL THEATRE
MA MUSICAL THEATRE

If you decide to become a student at the Royal Conservatoire of Scotland, you'll enjoy the nurturing and challenging environment you need to develop your talent to professional standards.

'This was a wonderful course, offering lots of exciting performance opportunities.'
Ishbel McFarlane
www.ishbelmcfarlane.com

'I attended this Drama School for 3 years and it was a wonderful experience. I learned a great deal about myself and other actors and I would recommend anyone who is interested in broadening and widening to register.'
Andrea Miller

THE ROYAL WELSH COLLEGE OF MUSIC AND DRAMA

CASTLE GROUNDS
CATHAYS PARK CF10 3ER
WWW.RWCMD.AC.UK
CCP MEMBERS: 366
COURSES:
BA (HONS) ACTING
MA ACTING FOR STAGE, SCREEN AND RADIO
MA MUSICAL THEATRE

The Royal Welsh College of Music & Drama, the National Conservatoire of Wales, and part of the Glamorgan Group, competes alongside an international peer group of conservatoires

47

and specialist arts colleges for the best students globally, enabling students to enter and influence the world of music, theatre and related professions.

'What a fantastic course. The training I have received over the past three years has been unforgettable. The course covers all the mediums of acting; theatre, radio, TV and Film, stage combat and more. The staff care so much for the training of each individual student and I could not have asked for more.'
Louisa Faye

'Fantastic training, fantastic college.'
Ed Williams

UNIVERSITY OF SALFORD
THE CRESCENT
SALFORD M5 4WT
WWW.SALFORD.AC.UK
CCP MEMBERS: 523
COURSES:
BA (HONS) PERFORMANCE: CONTEMPORARY PRACTICES
BA (HONS) PERFORMANCE: DRAMA AND THEATRE
Salford is an ambitious university at the heart of a fast-developing community. Our expertise is helping to transform individuals and communities through excellent teaching, research, innovation and engagement.

'I would highly recommend this course to anybody wanting to learn about the industry. A lot of the tutors are also working actors and can give great advice. There are also countless opportunities to perform with fantastic equipment available.'
Mary Murray

'Great course! It is for proactive actors though and not for people who want to be spoon fed. Prepares you for the reality of the industry and equips you to do-it-yourself, which is the way the technology and funding is going.'
Juel Stokes

BRISTOL OLD VIC THEATRE SCHOOL
1 - 2 DOWNSIDE ROAD
BRISTOL BS8 2XF
WWW.OLDVIC.AC.UK
CCP MEMBERS: 357
COURSES:
BA (HONS) PROFESSIONAL ACTING
MA PROFESSIONAL ACTING
Students on all Acting Courses are trained in: Voice; Vocal Exploration; Interpretation of Text; Movement (including Modern Dance, basic Ballet and Tap); Stage Combat - to British Academy of Dramatic Combat Certificate standard; Acting Techniques; Text Study; Singing; Improvisation; Audition Techniques; Musical Theatre; Radio Drama and Microphone Techniques; Television and Camera Techniques, also Commercials, Voice-overs, Dubbing, Autocue; Stage Management; Self-promotion / Marketing, Tax and Career Management.

'The best training an actor needs to start their career.'
Dilek Sengul
www.unitedagents.co.uk/dilek-sengul

'Bristol Old Vic Theatre School is a prestigious drama school with a strong reputation for excellent training in theatre, screen and radio acting. It prepares trainee actors for a diverse industry, with world class training in singing, dance, stage combat, voice and acting. It attracts acclaimed directors and practitioners to work with its students, including the likes of Sonia Fraser, Andrew Hilton and Maureen Scott.'
Elliot Chapman

48

Short Courses

Short-term courses are perfect for when you want to refresh, update or develop your skills. This is just a taster of the training providers out there - check online for your local coaching centres. Do keep in mind that many of the Drama Schools listed in the previous A-Z also offer short courses, in addition to those advertised regularly on the Casting Call Pro Noticeboard: **www.castingcallpro.com/uk/notices.php**.

THE ACADEMY OF CREATIVE TRAINING
BRIGHTON
WWW.ACTBRIGHTON.ORG

ACT attracts students of all ages and walks of life and enables people to realistically achieve their ambition of a career in the performing arts. Classes are in the evenings and at weekends so that students can continue to meet their working and/or domestic commitments whilst re-training.

THE ACTORS CENTRE
LONDON
WWW.ACTORSCENTRE.CO.UK

The Actors Centre was created by actors, for actors. For over 30 years we have provided ongoing training of the highest quality, giving actors the opportunity to enhance every aspect of their craft. We are unique in Europe: a place dedicated to developing professional actors by giving them the tools to develop themselves as artists and as business people in a highly competitive and rapidly changing industry.

THE ACTORS' GUILD
LONDON
WWW.ACTORSGUILD.CO.UK

The Actor at the very centre. From the artistic vision and management structure right the way through to the program of workshops which is created by the membership. We bring together key industry professionals, strict membership criteria and a low membership fee.

ACTORS' STUDIO
BUCKINGHAMSHIRE / LONDON
WWW.ACTORSSTUDIO.CO.UK

Based at the heart of the British Film Industry, Actors' Studio was formed in 2004 at Pinewood Studios by former Acting Agent Tim Kent. Actors' Studio offers training and networking courses/workshops for aspiring and professional actors at locations in Pinewood and also Central London.

THE ACTORS' TEMPLE
LONDON
WWW.ACTORSTEMPLE.COM

In less than a decade, The Actors' Temple has formed an 'enviable reputation as a place where students are free to be themselves' (The Stage, June 2011). The studio theatre on Warren Street offers not only exceptional training based on the principles of Sanford Meisner, but also the opportunity to become part of an ever-growing community of talented actors producing work of the highest calibre.

ACT UP
LONDON
WWW.ACT-UP.CO.UK

We are an independent organisation specialising in communication and acting training. We run short, part-time courses and bespoke, on-site training for people in business. Everyone involved in act up are very much working, established actors or industry practitioners; everything you will experience comes straight from the horse's mouth.

ACT UP NORTH
MANCHESTER / LIVERPOOL / LEEDS
WWW.ACTUPNORTH.COM
Founded in 2009 by UK Acting Coach Peter Hunt, ActUpNorth has grown to be one of the largest and most successful independent training programmes for actors outside London.

THE BRIDGE THEATRE TRAINING COMPANY
LONDON
WWW.THEBRIDGE-TTC.ORG
Every year people of all nationalities and backgrounds come to The Bridge to change their lives and become professional actors. If that's your dream, we're here to help you make it happen.

THE BRITISH ACADEMY OF STAGE & SCREEN COMBAT
WWW.BASSC.ORG
The British Academy of Stage & Screen Combat was founded in 1993 with the aim of improving the standards of safety, quality and training of stage combat and promoting a unified code of practice for the training, teaching and assessing of stage combat within the United Kingdom.

CITY LIT
LONDON
WWW.CITYLIT.AC.UK
City Lit is London's ultimate destination for

inspiring evening, daytime and weekend courses for adults. Each year we offer thousands of part-time courses, always trying to follow new trends and the passions and interests of our learners.

GILES FOREMAN CENTRE FOR ACTING
LONDON
WWW.GILESFOREMAN.COM
The Giles Foreman Centre for Acting (formerly the Caravanserai Acting Studio, based in Ladbroke Grove) is an exciting professional acting studio in the heart of London, housing some of the top coaches in the country in the disciplines of acting, movement, voice, improvisation and camera technique.

INTERNATIONAL SCHOOL OF SCREEN ACTING
LONDON
WWW.SCREENACTING.CO.UK
ISSA is a unique drama school dedicated to preparing actors for today's TV and Film Industry. Based within the prestigious 3 mills studios, we are in the heart of a creative and successful media village. The school is surrounded by a constant hive of activity with highly regarded film and TV programmes made within its secure and picturesque setting.

THE POOR SCHOOL
LONDON
WWW.THEPOORSCHOOL.COM
The Poor School aims to deliver the highest quality acting training for the lowest possible cost.

Chapter 2
Agents

Agents

Whilst it is by no means obligatory to get an agent as an actor, it is highly advisable. Agents deal with the business side of your career: negotiating financial deals, handling contracts, managing your diary, collecting your fees, and fighting your corner if anything goes wrong - allowing you to concentrate on what you do best. Good agents usually have excellent relationships with casting directors and are plugged in to the acting world, aware of what is in pre-production and what is currently casting so they can put you forward for jobs that are frequently not advertised publicly. In return they take a commission (usually 10-20%) from the work they get for you. Some larger agencies, and indeed some of the smaller successful ones, charge VAT on top of that.

Most agents work on a sole representation basis, but it is possible to have a main agent and a secondary, specialist agent for voiceover or commercial work. Note that some agents charge commission on ALL acting work you undertake (whether you get it through the agency or your own contacts) so do check the agency contract and terms of engagement before you sign on the dotted line. If this is the case, don't be tempted to hoodwink them by withholding details of acting work to avoid paying the commission. This is a rocky road that can lead to the break-up of the partnership. And of course Mr Inland Revenue takes a dim view of cash in hand work. Remember that you're still responsible for your own personal finances and filing your Annual Tax Return as a self-employed actor. There's more information about this in Chapter Four.

How to Get an Agent

First and foremost, there should be no joining fee for signing with an agency, and the actors' union Equity advises against those that charge upfront fees. All fees should be taken on a commission basis from work they obtain for you.

'For me, I wanted someone who I could see was hard working and as dedicated to their job as myself. I also wanted someone I could talk to and who understood the emotional rollercoaster of being an actor.'
Matt Downton
www.castingcallpro.com/uk/matt.downton

'Treat them like family and a teammate in your business of acting. I love my agent. They are just like me. Tenacious, hungry, and determined. Find one that matches your profile.'
Price Linsdey
www.pricelindsey.com

'Big is not necessarily best. You can get lost in a big agency and some big agents will give graduates a year to 'make it' and have no qualms about getting rid of them and getting in the next lot of graduates if they haven't. Look at the clients on an agent's website, see what kind of work they have done, don't be afraid to ask questions. Never go with an agent who has not seen you work, either onstage or via a showreel. Do your research about the agency, ask around, have a clear idea of what your niche is when you apply. Make your application concise and clear: pages of waffle and buttering up don't work!'
Fiz Marcus

Agents

© Rosie Still

'Start small and build up. Getting a big agent doesn't guarantee you'll get work. A smaller agent tends to be hungrier and will work for you.'
Frank Scantori

© Caroline Webster

'It's all about the relationship! You have to connect on a personal level. Keep on working and invite agents to see everything you do. It's their livelihood to 'discover' new talent and put them up for work. If you can make them money, they will plug away on your behalf. The biggest agents are not always the best ones for you. I was with an A-list agent early on in my career but they spent almost all their time looking after their A-list clients and I got kind of left out. Don't get me wrong, they were lovely and worked hard, its just that they were tied up so much with the big clients that they didn't have time to promote me as much. I moved to a smaller agency where they concentrated on me, best move I ever made.'
Craig Stevenson
www.craigstevenson.com

Being clear on your goals when researching an agent is vital – what do you want to achieve? Do you have particular ambitions in film, or theatre, or TV? Look at their client list – who do they also represent? Do they specialise in a specific area? How big are they – larger agencies may have a bigger reach, but smaller ones may be able to give you more individualised attention. Be aware that they may not wish to take you on if you're similar to an existing client to avoid the clashing of interests.

© Trevor Richards

'*Just write to agents if you are appearing in a play or are on TV. Ask them to come and see you performing. If you can, find out as much as you can about their agency. Find out who they have on their books and if they do not have anyone like you, point this out to them.*'
Phillip Law

© Desdemona Varon

'*Write a killer introductory letter, ultimately know your selling points, and casting potential – they are a business after-all. Why should they spend time with you?*'
Thomas O'Malley

© Claire Grogan

'*I just did lots of fringe plays and invited agents to come and see them. But if you go that route, then it's important that the play is worth doing for its own sake because there's no guarantee that agents are going to come or that they're going to take you on. It's all trial and error – even when you get an agent. I kissed a few frogs before I got one I was really happy with.*'
James Holmes

Once you've made a shortlist of agencies you'd like to approach, write to them with a covering letter, CV and headshot. The agency website should let you know if this should be done by post or email in the first instance. If you send your submission by post make sure you clearly mark your headshot (and showreel, if applicable) with your name and contact details. Always tailor your approach to individual agents: address your letter to a specific person, let them know why you'd be a good fit for them – and vice versa.

How to Write the Perfect Agent Letter

How to get Noticed, Signed and Cast - Fast!

THIS GUIDE WAS KINDLY WRITTEN FOR US BY ALREADYLABELLED.COM

The exact formula doesn't necessarily exist for writing the perfect letter to agents. It's not mathematics. However, there are simple things you can do, to drastically increase your chances of your letter being read, rather than becoming waste paper.

Know who you're writing to

Perhaps the most important piece of advice is to know exactly who you're sending your submission to. So much of the profession is about research, and sourcing somebody who you'd like to represent you is no different in terms of the way it should be approached. It's no use writing generic letters, you should really invest some valuable time into finding out more about the agency.

Get the balance right between formal and familiar

Remember, unless you know the person that you're writing to, they're an industry professional and they will not appreciate you making jokes or including gimmicks. Agents have all had submissions with tea bags included to 'soothe them while they read' and it is an instant turn-off. You should be polite and friendly but not overbearing or in any way pushy.

Make sure your photographs are up-to-date

This may sound obvious, but making sure that your 10x8 photographs are a true representation of your look is incredibly important. If you've lost weight over the last few years or drastically changed your hairstyle, invest some money into new headshots and refrain from writing to agents for a while. It's incredibly embarrassing to turn up to an interview and look nothing like the photo that you've sent them. Your look is probably one of the main reasons that they want to see you.

Keep the letter concise

It goes without saying that all good agents are incredibly busy people and they're working with people whom they already represent. Although they all have systems in place to monitor new submissions, if your letter is too long, it won't be read. There's nothing worse than opening a letter and revealing something akin to a dissertation beneath the envelope. Certainly write no more than 200 words and use an easily readable font at an appropriate size (12pt). You don't need to include your entire work history on your cover letter, as all of these credits appear on your CV.

If there is common ground, by all means talk about it

Having said above not to include credits on your CV, if you were working with one of the agent's clients on your latest project then this could be a terrific starting point in your letter: 'I was delighted to learn that you represent John Smith, who I recently collaborated with in the Donmar's production of A Midsummer Night's dream. We all had a brilliant time working on it...' Furthermore, if they represent other performers from the institution where you trained, include a sentence or two about that. More than anything else, it shows that you've bothered to look at their client list and that you've made professional associations with those you've worked with or trained alongside.

Consider different ways of presentation

This statement should be treated with caution. Glamourising letters with colour and illustrations, stickers and fancy artwork can appear

"Unless you know the person that you're writing to, they will not appreciate you making jokes or including gimmicks"

unprofessional and gimmicky. Try and avoid this at all costs. However, if you are appearing in a production that you'd like the Agent to consider coming to view, a professionally designed postcard might be an option. Companies print these at a relatively low cost and if you are unable to design it yourself, fiverr.com provide people who will do it for you for under £3.50. It gives the Agent less to read and digest and perhaps they'd be more inclined to pick up the diary and check their availability.

Already Labelled helps you get noticed, signed & cast – fast. They provide agent and casting director addresses, on labels, to save you having to write hundreds of addresses on envelopes when you're in a hurry. They also give your submissions a more professional and dynamic look. Stand out from the crowd and have industry professionals at your fingertips. Check out our blog for more free information about submitting to Agents & Casting Directors. **www.alreadylabelled.com**

A good way to start a dialogue with an agent is to invite them to see you perform. Drama schools invite agents to their graduation showcases, and there are also regular showcases in London venues that you have to apply to take part in – they can be expensive but are generally well-run and well-attended. If you don't have any upcoming performances let them know you can supply a showreel on request – again, check the submission guidelines as some agencies will only be able to accept showreels on DVD rather than a link to an online version.

Be aware that due to the sheer volume of interest agents receive, and the fact their main responsibility is to their existing clients, agents can't see every production, so be patient and don't be put off by a standard 'our lists are full' reply. Alternatively the agent may like you but, for a variety of reasons, you might not be suitable at that particular time. In both cases, keep in touch every now and again – send them an updated CV and headshot, or invite them to another production from time to time. Badgering them repeatedly to the point of irritation will do you no favours.

Our actors are agreed on one thing: communication with agents is key. Before signing meet up face to face and be clear and open about your goals. Once you're a client keep them posted with what you're working on and let them know if you're developing a new skill. Whether you end up having a close relationship with your agent, or see them more a business associate, what's vital is mutual trust and respect.

If you and your agent do part ways, check your contract for the notice period as you may still be required to pay commission for a period even though you might have left. Try to leave on good terms – the acting profession is swift-moving and you'll run into the same people time and again, so it makes good sense to maintain amicable relations.

Agency Representation Q&A with Brood Management

BRIAN PARSONAGE KELLY STARTED BROOD IN 2003, AFTER BEING ADMINISTRATOR ON THE CLASSICAL ACTING COURSE AT LONDON ACADEMY OF PERFORMING ARTS. BEFORE THAT HE WAS A BBC RADIO PRODUCER/PRESENTER.

Q. Are you always on the lookout for new talent? If not, how do you decide when to open your books?

Yes, we are always looking for new clients and welcome applications.

Q. What are the factors that help you decide to attend a graduate showcase?

To attend a showcase, we decide based on several factors:
• Whether we have time
• Whether we have seen good students from that course previously
• Whether we have received a friendly and warm welcome at past visits
• Whether graduates from that school have a high employment rate

Q. Are you also happy to attend performances or productions to see an actor's work? If so, how should they invite you and how much notice should they give?

We will occasionally go and see a show in which we don't already know someone, but time is so precious, and our own clients' shows come first. Realistically, Edinburgh apart, there are comparatively few shows we visit just because we are invited by an actor.

Q. Lots of advice given to actors suggests sending headshots and covering letters to agents directly – is this something you're open to? If so, should they contact you by telephone, email or post in the first instance?

We like to receive headshots and CVs by email, not by post, but do not appreciate every class member of an entire course writing to us separately.

Q. Are there common mistakes actors make when applying for representation?

Mistakes actors make when applying include, but are not limited to:

- Not visiting our website to see how to apply, then phoning to ask questions answered on the website
- Phoning to ask my name because someone has told them they should, insisting on having my surname and then not being able to spell it
- Sending the same email to every agent and not even bothering to conceal the fact
- Posting an application with an inadequate stamp
- Applying when they are not experienced or trained enough
- Sending huge attachments that don't open instantly

Q. How does an actor get the best out of the actor-agent relationship?

Easy: have a great personality, don't make basic mistakes, and be professional at all times. We send out a document to our people, 'How to be a good client'. It explains exactly what to do and not do.

Q. If you like someone but they're not suitable at the time, is it worth them keeping in touch?

If we like someone but for some reason we can't take them on at the time, we would ask them to come back to us. Generally though, if we like someone, we take them on then and there.

Q. How do you determine rates of commission for different production types? Do you take commission on work that actors find themselves?

Our commission is 10% stage and 15% screen. Some agents are 12.5% across the board, but we prefer to keep theatre jobs on a lower

"Edinburgh apart, there are comparatively few shows we visit just because we are invited by an actor"

commission rate. We do not charge VAT on top, as many agents do. All agents take commission on all jobs a client gets, regardless of origin, unless by special arrangement.

Q. What would be your top tips for actors seeking representation?

Don't be idealistic. Show business is just that – a business. Everyone wants to make money out of you, so when an agent advises you to do this or that to help your career, listen to them. They have the experience to know what sells, and sad as it may be, you are, to show business, just a product.

Many thanks to Brian Parsonage Kelly at Brood Management for taking the time to answer these questions. ***www.broodmanagement.com***

Getting the Best from an Actor-Agent Relationship

'I do everything that I can to equip myself for my career and remember that my agent is working for me. I respect them and value them and know that they know everything that I can do as an actor.'
Clare Cameron
www.clarecameron.com

'For me it's all about communication. If you are with an agency that is really big and busy all the time, chances are your level of communication will be less unless you are always getting auditions! Find out if the agent sends you breakdowns of the work they put you up for. Represent your agency well and don't turn up late for auditions with excuses – it's just horrible! Don't rely totally on your agent and make sure your agreement works for you. If you are a busy bee always generating work for yourself like me, then it's better to have a contract that says you don't have to pay any commission on work you find yourself.'
Tonia Daley-Campbell

'I have recently signed with a new agent and we have had very detailed talks about what I want and will do and he has outlined that which he feels he can do and requires from me. Communication is important: don't pester an agent – they are probably doing a lot on your behalf and don't need telling, but the odd call or email to let them know your movements and what you are doing to find work will help keep you in their scope. Always let your agent know your availability, nothing annoys them more than to get a casting only to find the actor can't make it.'
Andrew Fettes
www.andrewfettes.weebly.com

Agents

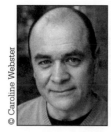

© Caroline Webster

'You can only expect your agent to work as hard on your behalf as you are prepared to work for yourself. Don't sit around and wait for the phone to ring. Get out there and be proactive. Network! Do classes! Don't forget to book out with your agent if you are not available. Keep them in the loop and speak to them at least once a week!'
Craig Stevenson
www.craigstevenson.com

Co-operative Agencies

If you're looking for an agent you might also want to consider a co-operative, where the actors run the agency themselves. Co-ops tend to have smaller client lists, and the actor can get a better understanding of, and connection to, the casting industry because they're also an agent. As a member of a co-op you'll be required to commit part of your time to working in the office, attending meetings and so on.

Most co-operative agencies are members of the Co-operative Personal Management Association. You can find out more about the CPMA via their website: **www.uk.coop**

Being a Member of an Actors' Co-operative Agency

THIS GUIDE WAS KINDLY WRITTEN FOR US BY ACTORS' CREATIVE TEAM

Actors' Creative Team was formed in 2001 and now has an average membership of 25 actors ranging in age from early 20s to early 60s. Some of us have had personal agents prior to joining the agency and some have come directly from drama school or a year or so later. While there is a common view in the acting world that only actors who couldn't get personal managers join co-operative agencies; and indeed some actors have used a co-op as a jumping off point to get personal management, those of us who stick with the co-op do so out of a belief that we are more involved in the industry and have 'hands-on' control of our careers.

We ask each member to work in our office 3-4 times a month, depending on how many people are out working. This enables us to have 2 people in the office so that we can cover phones, make submissions, take casting appointments, invoice for jobs, research new leads by talking to casting directors, producers or theatre, and check out new applications for membership. Being part of the administrative aspects of the industry in this way provides us with an insight to the structure of castings, relationships within the industry and the realistic expectations of those relationships.

This means that no matter how much acting work any of our members is getting at any given time, we are all regularly connected to the casting world and feel part of a team. We can always find out what jobs we have been submitted for; and we can be aware of the type of projects that come through and the level of work that is typical for the actors within the agency to expect. If any of us feels that what we are

"No matter how much acting work any of our members is getting, we are all regularly connected to the casting world and feel part of a team"

being submitted for is not the most suitable work, or that very few submissions are resulting in castings, we can address these concerns with our colleagues.

As individual members within the agency, we have very active and open communication which strengthens not only our sense of being part of a team but also of being supported as individual actors trying to find work. One of our newer members says: 'I feel I can call the agency anytime and whoever's in the office is always happy to be of help.' Our fortnightly meetings to discuss agency business also enable us to strengthen our professional relationships, exchange ideas and information, and learn about each others' skills, personalities and views in a way which can only enhance how we represent each other as agents.

We are aware that there can be a stigma against co-operative agencies simply because they tend not to have the weight that career agents at major agencies possess. However, many casting directors have said that they prefer to work with co-operatives because they are most proactive in finding and processing work for their clients. Certainly over the last decade we at Actors' Creative Team believe that we have built, and continue to develop, strong relationships with casting professionals; and have earned a solid and respected place in the industry.

Actors' Creative Team is a co-operative acting agency, established in 2001. With a client base of dynamic and focused actors between the ages of 20 and 60, we are able to offer a wealth of experience and talent to the film, television and theatre industries.
www.actorscreativeteam.co.uk

Going It Alone – the Business of Managing Yourself

© Stuart M Price

'Some people would say it's better to have ANY agent than no agent. Personally I don't agree. I got a good agent after leaving drama school, then unfortunately they went back to their old job so I've had to do it alone for nearly three years, and I've worked consistently. No one is going to work harder on your career than you. When you first start off you may be put up for jobs you could find yourself, so while you're struggling to pay the rent you're also paying up to 20% commission too. That said if you're lucky enough to get a good agent who works hard for you, they deserve to be paid. I think it's individual to every performer but I would say if you don't get an agent immediately develop your CV first, get in a good showcase at a good venue and then write to the agents that are in your league and you genuinely want to work for. Remember it's your money and your career.'

Bryony Tebbutt
www.bryonytebbutt.com

Don't forget there's no set route into a successful acting career and an agent is by no means the absolute be all and end all. Indeed some people prefer the autonomy and control they experience in going it alone, not to mention the commission rates you save yourself! We asked some CCP members who work without an agent for some tips and advice about managing their careers solo.

Invest in Your Own Career

THIS GUIDE WAS WRITTEN BY DOUGLAS BROWN

© Ivor Houlker

So without having an agent, it's easy to presume you don't know where you're going, or that you aren't good enough. These are some of the presumptions you will be faced with as an actor/actress working independently. Having an agent isn't the be all and end all of having a successful career in acting. For me, the choice came from knowing what I wanted whilst also knowing the types of roles I wanted to aim for and explore. Most importantly, the pressure of being in control of my own career is my biggest motivation to strive towards success.

Since I began acting full time (more hours maybe than a full time job), I have been racking up the credits and getting more material for my showreel. I work hard and put the hours in because I know what I want and where I want to be, and what it takes to get there. Ultimately, I'm constantly doing what I love and what makes me happy, because that's what I want from my life. Going it alone can make you feel proud of what you are doing. After all, it's all your own doing and work you've put in, no one else will never have as much vested interest in your career as you will.

However, what needs to be remembered is that you are your own brand. You represent yourself and are in control of your own image. One huge element to remember when representing yourself is to NETWORK NETWORK NETWORK. The more contacts you have, and the more you get yourself out there the better. Personally, I hate the whole business card venture (easily lost, forced to accept, not personal),

"The more contacts you have, and the more you get yourself out there the better"

69

instead I opt more in the way of asking for numbers and emails to stay in contact. Of course, in this day and age social media is becoming a huge method of contacting people ... take advantage of it.

My final tips and advice, to all my fellow individuals going it alone, are to network and communicate with people. Someone, somewhere may see your potential and give you the opportunity to push you forward. Educate and explore new roles, to ensure you can see what works and what does not. Finally, never lose the love for what you are doing and wanting to achieve. That drive and passion will get you through the rejections, criticisms, and slow days without work. It will give you the encouragement to go above and beyond your own expectations. So don't give up, and work hard.

THIS GUIDE WAS WRITTEN BY ROBERT HARPER

© Claire Cage

First, let me just dispel the myth that 'without an agent I won't get any work'. It's simply not true. At least, it's not true as long as you make the best use of your time when you're not working. Don't get me wrong, with a good agent you can get seen for jobs that you might not otherwise, and they can certainly help negotiate contracts and ensure you get the right fees. But with the right attitude you can do it all for yourself if you're out there on your own.

In my early years as an actor, I was desperate to get myself an agent right out of college. At the time I knew nothing about how to look for my own work, network or get my name out there. I got one luckily, and it worked in a fashion for me for a while, then I moved to London, things got exciting, and I changed agents.

As it stands now, after taking a break from acting for a few years, I came back to it and decided that going it alone for a while wouldn't be such a bad thing. Finding opportunities for myself and using online tools like social media and Casting Call Pro to network with other creatives, brought its rewards.

You can't sit around and wait for it, you have to put the time in and treat it like a full time job, especially when you're 'resting'. Because, believe me, if you rest too much, you're going to miss out.

Robert's website is **www.robert-harper.co.uk**

THIS GUIDE WAS WRITTEN BY ROSIE THORPE HEADSHOT © CLAIRE GROGAN

© Claire Cage

I am an actress who has worked pretty much consistently for the last 3 years, without an agent. I currently have a voiceover agent but I find acting work myself.

Since finishing my actor training at The Arts University, Bournemouth in 2010 I went straight into an 11 month tour of Germany with White Horse Theatre. I then went out to Italy to teach kids drama for a week (a job found through CCP) where I made a friend for life, David Hutchinson, Artistic Director of Sell-A-Door Theatre Company. He very kindly offered me a role in their Christmas play in 2011, A Christmas Carol. The Managing Director of Sell-A-Door Theatre Company, Phillip Rowntree, saw me in this production and asked me to audition for a tour he was directing out in Austria with Vienna's English Theatre. I then spent six months touring Austria in 2012. When this tour ended I went back to Sell-A-Door to Assistant Produce their West End Musical, Seussical, and now after 4 months working on the production side I am back performing in their current tour, 1984. Representing yourself means you not only build up a host of contacts but a lot of solid friendships, and I owe a lot of my career to those guys.

"I feel it is fully possible to represent yourself, if you are open-minded to opportunities and are persistent with applications and auditions"

Agents

So far, I have made a career out of acting through networking, patience and hard work. I feel it is fully possible to represent yourself, if you are open-minded to opportunities and are persistent with applications and auditions. Always chase up an opportunity; never let it slide as the worst someone can say is no

Thanks to Douglas, Robert and Rosie for sharing their experience and advice.

A-Z of Agencies

There are a large number of agencies out there and no easy way of knowing which one would be right for you. Do your research - read their websites, see who their other clients are, ask around for recommendations from other actors. To help you get started, we've broken down some of the agency information available on Casting Call Pro into different listings. The following are by no means exhaustive, and you can go to **www.castingcallpro.com/uk/asearch.php** to find out more. All figures are correct at the time of going to press.

Top 10 Agencies representing the largest number of Casting Call Pro members

ASH PRODUCTIONS LIVE LTD
WEST NORWOOD
WWW.ASHPRODUCTIONSLIVELTD.COM
CCP MEMBERS: 77
ASH Productions LIVE - Personal Management represents and mentors a diverse range of experienced artists and new talent working closely with every individual to take their career to new levels.

BYRON'S MANAGEMENT
LONDON
WWW.BYRONSCASTING.CO.UK
CCP MEMBERS: 65
Byron's Management has been established for over fifteen years. We are sole management agents. We represent our clients in theatre, film, television and commercials. The Byron's team pride themselves on representing extremely talented and professional actors who continue to build on Byron's strong reputation within the industry.

FABNEWFACES
LONDON
WWW.FABNEWFACES.CO.UK
CCP MEMBERS: 56
Fabnewfaces is a great and reliable agency. We support new faces, as well as established Models and Actors.

JOHN DOE MANAGEMENT
LONDON
WWW.JOHNDOEMGT.COM/
CCP MEMBERS: 65
John Doe Management is a boutique agency that represents a select and diverse range of talented actors in the commercial, film and television industry. We deliberately keep our client numbers low to ensure quality and a great working relationship with everyone we represent. We understand the strengths and abilities of all our artists and strive to ensure they reach their full potential.

Agents

K TALENT ARTIST MANAGEMENT LTD
LONDON
WWW.KTALENT.CO.UK
CCP MEMBERS: 87
K Talent was originally set up by Kris Lythgoe as part of the K Entertainments Group in 2004 and has since grown and developed into a well established Agency. K Talent represents clients in all fields of the entertainment industry, including Television, Film, Theatre Drama, Musical Theatre, Commercials, Music and Endorsements. There are no age restrictions and graduates from accredited training establishments are also encouraged.

LEADING ROLE AGENCY LTD
WEST MIDLANDS
WWW.LEADINGROLEAGENCY.CO.UK
CCP MEMBERS: 55
Leading Role film and Television Management is a vibrant new company representing UK's brightest acting talent.

MACFARLANE DOYLE ASSOCIATES
CHESHIRE
WWW.MACFARLANEDOYLE.COM
CCP MEMBERS: 69
MacFarlane Doyle is a dynamic agency representing actors and other creative workers in the entertainment industry. The agency was founded by Ross MacFarlane and Perry Doyle in 2009. Our aim is quite simply to provide a dedicated and personal service to our clients, and to the casting professionals who use our expertise. We believe passionately in what we are doing and aim to approach the development of the careers of our clients in an intelligent, innovative and candid manner.

NIC KNIGHT MANAGEMENT
LONDON
WWW.NICKNIGHTMANAGEMENT.COM
CCP MEMBERS: 102
Nic Knight doesn't believe in A or B lists, ignoring calls or agents behaving like drama queens. As a company, we treat our clients and contacts in the industry as we could wish to be treated. Above all, our clients know that if they are on our books it's because we believe in them and we're promoting them every way we can.

SIMON & HOW ASSOCIATES
LONDON
WWW.SIMON-HOW.COM
CCP MEMBERS: 94
SIMON & HOW ASSOCIATES are a new, exciting and vibrant actor's agency founded in 2007 by company directors, Simon Penn and Samantha How. Having worked with leading talent agencies in the past, and with over 20 years collective experience in the industry, they are now building a solid reputation for representing a diverse list of talented, up and coming actors for theatre, film, television, commercials and photographic jobs.

TONY YOUNG CASTING
LANCASHIRE
WWW.TONYYOUNGCASTING.CO.UK/
CCP MEMBERS: 71
A theatrical agent dedicated in providing talent for Film, TV and Theatre.

Top 10 PMA Agencies representing the highest number of Casting Call Pro members

Some agents are members of the Personal Managers Association, the leading professional body for talent agencies in the UK. You can find out more about the PMA here via their website: **www.thepma.com**

APM ASSOCIATES

BOREHAMWOOD
WWW.APMASSOCIATES.NET
CCP MEMBERS: 33

APM Associates was founded by Linda French in 1989 and has grown into one of the leading personal management agencies in the UK. APM Associates successfully represent clients in all fields of the entertainment industry, including Television, Film, Theatre, Musical Theatre, Voice-overs, Commercials and Dance.

BWH AGENCY LTD

LONDON
WWW.THEBWHAGENCY.CO.UK
CCP MEMBERS: 28

The BWH Agency Ltd was formed in 2004 by Andrew Braidford, Lisa Willoughby, Joe Hutton and Bill Petrie. Based on honesty and a good old fashioned ethic of hard work, we pride ourselves on providing an efficient and personal service to our clients and colleagues.

GALLOWAYS

LONDON
WWW.GALLOWAYSAGENCY.COM
CCP MEMBERS: 35

Established in 1991 as JGM, we relaunched in 2011 as Galloways and represent a select but diverse list of actors for theatre, television, film and radio, with a strong musical theatre list. Galloways are a small, close-knit team who focus on the individual needs of our actors.

IMPERIUM MANAGEMENT

LONDON
WWW.IMPERIUM-MANAGEMENT.COM
CCP MEMBERS: 71

Imperium represents a diverse and select group of actors within all areas of film, television and theatre. We carefully pick and support talent with an interesting edge and diverse range of styles, as well as professional, warm personalities. It is paramount to us that our artists are great to work with, and we believe this has played an important part in our growing reputation within the industry.

MRS JORDAN ASSOCIATES

LONDON
WWW.MRSJORDAN.CO.UK
CCP MEMBERS: 23

Mrs Jordan Associates represents a small number of clients who range from those who have performed at the RSC, The Royal National Theatre, Shakespeare's Globe, The Old Vic and in leading television roles to recent graduates.

Agents

NICOLA ROBERTS MANAGEMENT

Surrey

WWW.NICOLAROBERTSMANAGEMENT.COM

CCP MEMBERS: 32

Nicola Roberts Management is a dynamic theatrical talent agency with a fresh approach to representing actors in all areas of the industry. We pride ourselves on fully supporting our actors with professional advice, encouragement and genuine empathy, We aim to provide a friendly, personable service whilst delivering the highest quality professionalism. Regular meetings and ongoing communication ensure that, together, we build a strong partnership based on trust and honesty so we are best placed to drive your specific career goals forward.

PAUL BYRAM ASSOCIATES

London

WWW.PAULBYRAM.COM

CCP MEMBERS: 52

Paul Byram Associates is a personal management company and talent agency in London with industry links in Sydney, Australia. We aim to provide our clients with more access to better quality casting briefs and job opportunities. We believe in providing the level of service most people only dream of and we commit to doing this every single day. PBA are equally committed to Casting Directors and industry professionals to ensure the best and most appropriate talent for the job is proposed.

PELHAM ASSOCIATES

Brighton

WWW.PELHAMASSOCIATES.CO.UK

CCP MEMBERS: 29

Representing actors of the highest quality for casting in all branches of the media.

ROBERT KELLY ASSOCIATES

London

WWW.ROBERTKELLYASSOCIATES.COM

CCP MEMBERS: 28

Launched by Robert Kelly, RKA has grown to become one of the leading talent agencies in the UK with strong US links. RKA represents fresh new talent as well as seasoned actors and casting directors who have won Olivier Awards, Evening Standard Awards, British Soap Awards, Critics Circle Awards and Theatregoers' Choice Awards. With over 20 years combined of experience, Robert and Helen assisted by Will pride themselves on providing personalised and professional services to clients.

STEVE NEALON ASSOCIATES

London

WWW.STEVENEALONASSOCIATES.CO.UK

CCP MEMBERS: 39

The agency was founded by Steve Nealon, who has over twenty years experience working in the industry both in the UK and Ireland. Covering Film, Television, Commercials & Theatre, we provide a wide cross section of experienced actors, strong graduates and talented, dedicated young people. We are discerning with our submissions, reliable and straightforward with our actors and clients and have a strong understanding of the casting process. SNA is a member of the Personal Managers Association.

Top 10 Co-operative Agencies representing the highest number of Casting Call Pro members

ACTORS' CREATIVE TEAM
LONDON
WWW.ACTORSCREATIVETEAM.CO.UK
CCP MEMBERS: 17
Actors' Creative Team is a co-operative acting agency, established in 2001. With a client base of dynamic and focused actors between the ages of 20 and 60, we are able to offer a wealth of experience and talent to the film, television and theatre industries.

THE ACTORS' FILE
LONDON
WWW.THEACTORSFILE.CO.UK
CCP MEMBERS: 16
The Actors File is a small boutique Co-operative Personal Management created 28 years ago. As one of the first waves of co-operatives in Britain it was at the forefront of the changing face of representation. We do our utmost to stay there, remaining competitive and accessible. Started by 5 actors (2 of whom are still with us) we now represent around 20 actors covering a wide range of types and skills.

CITY ACTORS MANAGEMENT
LONDON
WWW.CITYACTORS.CO.UK
CCP MEMBERS: 20
City Actors Management has long been one of London's leading co-operative agencies. Since 1982 we have been providing the industry with a wide variety of trained actors with stage, television, film and radio experience.

CRESCENT MANAGEMENT
LONDON
WWW.CRESCENTMANAGEMENT.CO.UK
CCP MEMBERS: 11
We supply professional, trained and talented actors for the stage and screen.

DENMARK STREET MANAGEMENT
LONDON
WWW.DENMARKSTREET.NET
CCP MEMBERS: 17
Established in 1985, Denmark Street Management has developed over the years to become one of the UK's leading co-operative agencies - specialising in providing highly skilled professional actors for theatre, film, television, commercials and radio.

INSPIRATION MANAGEMENT
LONDON
WWW.INSPIRATIONMANAGEMENT.ORG.UK
CCP MEMBERS: 17
Inspiration Management was formed in 1986 with the aim of giving its members control over the direction and purpose of their careers, gaining an insight into the way the industry works and providing a sense of camaraderie: each actor working within a group of others, to further their own and their colleagues' careers.

Agents

NORTH OF WATFORD
WEST YORKSHIRE
WWW.NORTHOFWATFORD.COM
CCP MEMBERS: 15
North Of Watford Actors' Agency is one of the longest running co-operative agencies in the country. In 2009 we celebrated 25 years in the industry. We were established in 1984 by a group of actors living in the North of England who were keen to manage their careers. They worked to gain a greater understanding of the industry and each other, enabling them to provide clients with the best possible service. Their ethos continues today.

NORTHONE MANAGEMENT
LONDON
WWW.NORTHONE.CO.UK
CCP MEMBERS: 14
NorthOne Management was founded as an actors agency in 1986. Since then its founding members have moved on, but bequeathed a wealth of accumulated experience, which the current members enjoy.

ROSEBERRY MANAGEMENT
LONDON
WWW.ROSEBERYMANAGEMENT.COM
CCP MEMBERS: 21
Rosebery Management was established in 1984 by the late Nona Alexander and is now one of the UK's most prestigious co-operative agencies.

STAGE CENTRE MANAGEMENT
LONDON
WWW.STAGECENTRE.ORG.UK
CCP MEMBERS: 20
Stage Centre Management is a cooperative actors agency based in North London. Formed in 1982, the agency represents around 25 actors from all areas of the industry. Stage Centre members regularly appear in the West End and in feature films, on UK and European theatre tours, and on television and in commercials.

Chapter 3
An Actor's Essentials

Headshots

© Claire Newman-Williams

'With headshots it's about you jumping out of the picture above all of the rest. This requires research on finding the photographer who has a good reputation and works with you to help you feel comfortable.'
Debbie Bridge

© Claire Grogan

Headshots must look different – there's no point having a few headshots which are essentially the same but from slightly different angles. Don't be frightened to show your teeth in a smile. Wear clothing and choose hairstyles which are indicative of your casting types. Most important – choose a good photographer who is a proper headshot photographer, not a glamour photographer!'
Linda Large

© Nicholas Dawkes

'I have to like the photographer's previous work, they have to be reasonably priced, and I want to look like me on a good day, not airbrushed to distraction.'
Alex Scott Fairley

The industry standard for acting photos is a 10 x 8" (25 x 20cm) headshot taken by a professional photographer. The headshot will usually take in your head and the top of your shoulders but shouldn't include the rest of your body. The pose should be natural and straight to camera, clearly displaying your entire face.

There are a variety of different elements to be taken into consideration with headshots: should you get black and white shots or colour? How do you choose a photographer? How long will the session be? What should you wear? Is it better to have natural or artificial lighting? How many final images will you get? How much should you be paying?

Overleaf actors headshot photographer Michael Wharley explains the dos and don'ts when it comes to headshots.

Take Control of Your Headshots

MICHAEL WHARLEY
P H O T O G R A P H Y

THIS GUIDE WAS KINDLY WRITTEN BY MICHAEL WHARLEY

Knock-out headshots remain as important today as when actors first started using them in the 1910s, says 'top theatre photographer' (The Stage) Michael Wharley, but with the arrival of colour, changes in online casting tools, and digital media advances, it's vital to make your headshots really work for your career.

What makes a headshot?
• Simply, a head and shoulders shot, eyes/face to camera, in a 10 x 8 size. Historically B&W.
• It must be truthful: says Pippa Harrison, Head of Client Relations at Spotlight: 'Your photos absolutely must look like you.' Casting directors want the 'you' who auditions to look like the 'you' in the photo.
• But headshots are also an actor's branding, so truthful doesn't mean dowdy: says TV, film and commercial casting director Janis Jaffa:

Subtly suggesting playing range via clothing, lighting and emotional choices in a modern headshot portfolio © Michael Wharley 2013

'Headshots need je ne sais quoi, something that makes [casting professionals] stop and look.'

What modern trends do you need to know about?
- In a survey conducted by myself and CCP, 96% of casting directors said they believe the headshot will remain important in the future of casting. BUT ...
- The casting process prior to audition is now largely handled online. The old idea of the single 'killer headshot' is being replaced by online headshots portfolios. These let you show casting directors the full range of your casting at the click of a mouse.
- Colour is in. Have one dedicated B&W shot, but the rest of your portfolio should be colour.
- Use the flexibility of your web-based CV to subtly showcase different sides of your casting - 3-6 photos makes a great portfolio.
- Hard copy prints are sometimes needed, but headshots are primarily digital in 2013.

When do you need headshots?
- If you're seeking professional acting work and for any reputable casting service. As James Hopson of Pippa Ailion Casting (Wicked, Legally Blonde and more), observes; 'they are the most important marketing tool for an actor'.
- You don't need headshots to apply to drama school. They are professional promotional tools.

How do I choose a photographer?
Check out the list at **www.castingcallpro.com/uk/psearch.php**: with so many great headshot photographers around, it really is a buyer's market, so do your research and consider:
- Session Time: 1 hour, 2 hours or more? It might be tempting to go for the shortest time, but it can often take a while to relax, especially in your first session.
- Natural or studio-lit: either is good, both is best, but make sure you know what you'll be getting.
- Cost of retouched prints: 1-4 will normally be included, but extras will cost £15-25 each. Unedited shots will make you look amateurish.

"Above £300, you are probably paying a premium for the photographer's reputation"

- Digital or Film: digital gives more freedom to explore and you can have colour or B&W shots.
- Colour or B&W: you definitely need the option of colour.
- Gut feeling: narrow it down to 2-3 photographers whose style, approach and price suit, then go with your instinct.

How much should I pay?
- Based on current UK trends, a session can cost anything from £50 to £580!
- You can sometimes get good shots at knock-down prices, but to ensure industry-standard photos and a decent length of time with a good photographer, expect to spend £150 or more.
- Above £300, you are probably paying a premium for the photographer's reputation.

What should I wear for the session?
- Take an array of contrasting plain tops, of different colours, necklines and textures; your photographer will help you choose which to use to get the most variety.
- For example: a black round or V-neck t-shirt, a vest top, a white long-sleeved tee, a coloured thin or chunky-knit jumper, a white shirt, a jacket and shirt, a coat with a high collar, a leather jacket, a hoody.
- Wear make-up as if you're going to an interview or audition, not a night out – these are promotional photos, not model shots.
- For women: light foundation, possibly blusher, and mascara / eyeliner.
- For men: rugged often looks best, but less is more if you do use make-up.
- Have any hair new dos done a couple of days before the session, so you grow out the 'salon look'.

- Don't plan a series of specific 'character' looks: headshots should subtly suggest aspects of your casting to casting professionals, e.g. a suit and tie can look specifically corporate, a suit and open-necked shirt can read lots of ways.

How can I get the most out of the session?
- Beforehand: think carefully about your casting types, how casting directors might perceive you and the different ways you'd like to be seen.
- Adrian Jeckells, principal at the London School of Musical Theatre, believes the successful modern actor 'assesses him or herself as a commercial entity' - so try to articulate the ways you'd like to be seen, then be ready to share with your photographer.
- Get lots of sleep and eat healthily in the few weeks before your session. Photoshop can take away spots, but it can't create a sense of vitality and well-being.
- During: treat your session like a trip to the hairdresser, not the dentist. Brief your photographer on your casting types, ask to see shots as the session progresses, don't be afraid to say what you like and don't like. You'll get better shots.
- Relax! Few people like being photographed, but the less tense you are the more yourself you'll appear in the shots.

How should I choose my final photos?
- Get feedback from as many people as possible: your peers, tutors and friendly industry contacts – it'll help you choose shots that fit your casting types / career ambitions, instead of the shots that make you look 'nicest'.
- Choose a selection of shots showcasing believable facets of your casting, across your playing range.

"Get feedback from as many people as possible: your peers, tutors and friendly industry contacts"

Anything else?

- Headshots are just one part of marketing yourself effectively as an actor.
- Your headshot is your business branding, so use it as a profile picture on any social media site you use for professional purposes – whether it's LinkedIn, Twitter, Facebook or others ...
- Copyright – make sure to credit your photographer wherever you use your headshots. Almost all will retain copyright and grant you the right to use photos for professional promotional purposes.

*Michael Wharley is a London-based actors headshot photographer and a 'leading voice on headshots and digital trends in the industry' (The Stage). He leads 'Take Control of Your Headshots' seminars for drama schools. Visit his site at **www.michaelwharley.com** and read his blog for industry insights **www.wharleywords.co.uk***

Showreels

© Alex Rumford

'Showreels should always be a work in progress.'
Will Harrison-Wallace
www.castingcallpro.com/uk/will.harrison-wallace

These days you might have a great headshot and CV, but your showreel is 'moving picture evidence' of your abilities as a performer and as such it's arguably one of the most important elements in the actor's toolkit. A CV and headshot might get someone's attention, but they can only provide part of the picture, and it's here that your showreel can play a vital role in taking you from a 'maybe' to a 'definite' in the casting director's eyes. If you're applying for representation, an agent is also very likely going to want to see your showreel as it's a quick and easy way for them to see what you can do as a performer.

Showreels are usually created from clips from previous work that showcase your ability as an actor. They should always be kept pacey, clean and relevant. Think about how many showreels a casting directors will watch for the average casting – they definitely do not have the time to watch a 6 minute video from start to finish! For this reason the first 30 seconds of your showreel are particularly important – some people like to include a short montage of their work so whoever is watching can get an overview of your past work and abilities, others prefer to open with a long close up or headshot still. It's also important that your showreel focuses on you playing characters you're likely to get cast as, so play to your strengths. Too much versatility can make it difficult for a casting director to picture you in a role. Lastly, don't forget that your name and contact details should be clearly visible at the start and end of your showreel.

Ideally you should have both DVD copies and streaming versions of your completed showreel which can be uploaded to websites and video hosting services such as YouTube or Vimeo. With the former it's important to think about the packaging too - make sure both the DVD and the box are clearly labelled with your name and contact number. You might even want to include your headshot on the DVD and/or DVD case. Make sure you also take into account the cost of having duplicate DVDs made when selecting a showreel provider. Internet-friendly streaming versions could be in a variety of formats (.avi, .mp4, .wmv are just some examples) but a typical file size for a 2-3 minute showreel is about 6MB.

© Claire Grogan

'I like to edit my showreel every 2 years. It must be short (3 minutes is long enough) and must only include material of good production quality, and definitely do not include home-movie footage or stage work. Keep each clip short. Make sure you show yourself, keep the appearance of scene partners to a minimum.'
Linda Large

© Carl Proctor

'The headshot is your gateway to attention and the showreel is the first post. There is nothing more irritating than seeing an actor who looks too different to their head shot or to watch a showreel that is too long. Three minutes is the maximum, bearing in mind that most people will become bored after 30 seconds.'
Carrie Cohen

© Vincent Abbey

'I would recommend that actors update their showreels annually, depending on the work they can generate over that time. Your work is only going to improve, so look for ways to insert your best work into a new showreel at regular intervals!'
Amir Rahimzadeh
www.33films.co.uk

© Jon Purcell

'If it has cheap looking footage, bad sound, and is bad visually it reflects badly on your professionalism and does you no favours. Sorry, most people do judge by this and even if they don't, if it's hard, difficult or disturbing to watch it's easier to move on.'

Sara Dee
www.castingcallpro.com/uk/sara.dee

Like headshots, showreels are an investment and as such there are lots of factors to think about: how long should your showreel be? What should you include? What if you don't yet have enough suitable content? How are they put together?

It can all seem a bit overwhelming but following the advice overleaf from The Actor's One Stop Shop can help you get the most of of your showreel.

Getting the Perfect Showreel

THIS GUIDE WAS KINDLY WRITTEN BY THE ACTOR'S ONE STOP SHOP

A showreel is probably the most powerful marketing tool you can have. Think about it, a friend may go on about how wonderful an actor is in this or that movie for months, but it's only when you actually see the movie that you can judge for yourself the strength of their performances.

From a casting perspective, setting up auditions is hard work and you can only really see about twenty five actors in a day, but with showreels you can see a hundred plus - and the fact that you're seeing performances rather than just social chin wagging leads to a more meritorious system where people can be cast primarily for their talent. Then there's the agent angle. If you're without an agent then you'll want one, and if you're with an agent then you'll want a better one. Either way they'll need to see what they're buying into: how can they represent you if they don't know what you can do?

So now you're sold. You want a showreel but it all seems rather complicated. In fact, it's actually very simple. Let's start at the base line: Do you have material from past films? If the answer is yes, then obviously you'd like that work to feature on your showreel. If not, the way to go is to shoot something from scratch. Let's take each case one at a time.

1. Edited from existing material showreels
First of all you need to sit down and review your existing work, making notes of your best scenes and using your video player's counter to note where they start and end. You'll want at most 3 clips from any particular production, and no more than 14 clips in total from all of your productions.

"Until you see just how powerful editing is in the hands of a good editor you won't really appreciate what can be achieved"

Then these clips are loaded onto a computer in an editing suite and carved down to a pacy and interesting showreel lasting between 3 and 4 minutes. What could be easier?

As regards cost it'll be by the hour. Some facilities offer 'all in' prices but then say 'up to x number of hours and then it'll be by the hour', so it's the same thing really. If you can't go above a certain price then tell the editor beforehand. If they're experienced they should be able to keep to it, though be aware that if you'd like them to do that they'll probably need to have quite a free reign on the showreel.

A common worry is that an actor's material is very weak and they're waiting for stuff. Don't worry, until you see just how powerful editing is in the hands of a good editor you won't really appreciate what can be achieved. Low budget and student films are often badly put together, but re-cutting, editing to reduce other characters and adding music can all give even the most uninspiring scene unbelievable muscle. It's a bit like what can be achieved with airbrushing photos – spots, wrinkles all gone! Beautiful tan and alluring eyes guaranteed! Editing is just as powerful.

So that promised copy of a film where you had a strong role that you've now been waiting for months to receive? Our advice is don't wait. Get something together now. If you go to a professional outfit they should keep your showreel so that new credits can be easily added, like you do with your CV. It makes an incredible difference when casting directors and agents are able to see your moving image and you don't want to have delayed, even a few months, only discover the clip you've been waiting for is less than hoped.

In terms of how many good scenes you need the answer is very simple: just one. If we hear you interacting with another character in just one scene then the other scenes may not even need words, their presence serves to strengthen your body of experience or the quality of productions you've been in.

But supposing you simply haven't been on camera enough, or the footage you do have is a bit below par? That's where the might of 'Shot-from-scratch' comes in.

2. Shot from scratch showreels

Again it's all very simple. Scenes are shot, edited and then put together on a showreel, so it looks as if they came from produced films. The end result appears like an edited from existing material showreel.

If you go to a company that can supply you with suitable scripts, actors and a director and who are prepared to produce the showreel, then it should be all very easy and even enjoyable - with a real chance to expand your acting talent into the bargain. One of the key things to avoid is the temptation to direct yourself. Characters are always more three dimensional and interesting under the guidance of a professional, experienced drama director and they'll give you honest feedback about what works and what doesn't, as well as what's feasible to shoot on your budget.

These scenes can be integrated with existing work, or can be used as a single scene by itself. One actor reported back a few months ago that he'd just been cast in a central role in a feature film based from a single simple scene.

When it comes to showreels we could go on for hours: UK format, USA format, splash montages, attention spans, musical flows, lyrical interaction between credits, establishment of primary character, use of action material, gluing section techniques, use of model style shots, target markets and so on, and on, and on ... Which is exactly what you might expect from a company who can in all likelihood claim to have made more showreels than anyone on the planet! There's a lot to it, but concentrate on the points and advice listed above and you'll be well on your way to putting together the most powerful tool in your professional acting arsenal: your showreel. Good luck!

The Actor's One Stop Shop is the longest established and most experienced specialist showreel company the UK has to offer. Still bristling with enthusiasm, fresh ideas and creativity for every showreel produced. **www.actorsone-stopshop.com**

Voicereels

If you're interested in working as a voiceover artist, you're going to need a voicereel: a 2-3 minute audio clip that showcases your vocal abilities. Is your unique selling point your clear, booming voice? Does your ability to go from cartoonishly crazy to sensual and seductive in 60 seconds flat set you apart from the others? Perhaps your strongest skill is in how you interact with your clients, recognising their needs, and using your voice to help them meet their goals.

Similar to a showreel, think about the sort of work you want to undertake. If you're a versatile artist, voicereels are great places to show off this ability - but remember, casting directors don't want to plough through hours of audio to get the voice they need, so think about creating a number of tailored voicereels with titles such as 'Commercial', 'Corporate' and 'Drama'.

Everything You Need to Know about Voicereels

THIS GUIDE WAS KINDLY WRITTEN BY TIM O'DONOGHUE, SOUND ENGINEER AT ANGELL SOUND

Surely a producer can hear what I sound like on the phone. Why do I need a voicereel?
A reel really helps to show that you are capable of delivering a finished product. It lets a producer judge what your voice sounds like in the right context and proves that you are capable of handling yourself in a recording environment.

Right, I've booked an appointment at a studio. What should I prepare?
This depends on the type of reel. For a Commercial reel typically we're looking for six scripts showcasing different types of read plus a short piece of narrative to show what your undirected voice is like. The six scripts can be picked from TV or radio, but radio scripts tend to work better in an audio-only reel for obvious reasons so avoid TV scripts with sight gags. Listen out for products that you can genuinely imagine your voice selling. A good engineer can help you with suggestions in the session, but it is important to think about this yourself before you get in the studio - if you have a clear idea of what type of voice you are and what type of work you are looking to get then you are more likely to succeed!

Should a voicereel be a collage of previous work, or should I focus on producing new material at my session?
I've often been asked to include bits of commercial work that has been on air in reels. Provided you've cleared it with the agency and it's not too old I wouldn't necessarily advise against as long as it sends the right message. In general though, you should try to make the reel as up to date as possible. A whole reel of paid work from ten years ago probably won't do you any good!

What happens in the average voicereel recording session?

The average commercial reel recording session takes a couple of hours, sometimes a little more. You might expect to have a quick discussion about the scripts you've chosen with the engineer and then get straight into the recording. If the engineer is directing and producing the reel for you, you'll find it's partly an organic process as it will usually take a few reads for them to get a feel for what each you are capable of. You'll take direction, the engineer will give you advice on intonation, pace and emphasis. You might be asked to do a script in a number of ways, you might even drop a script if it isn't working. Depending on the scripts that you have chosen, you might be introduced to different mic techniques or be asked to read along with a music track to get the right feel.

Do I need to bring my own music?

Usually the engineer will provide the music.

I've got this amazing little clip from an audio drama I was in. Does it matter that there's another voice there?

I wouldn't tend to include this sort of thing in a commercial reel, but obviously a drama reel could potentially benefit from some recent paid work so it might be worth considering. Make sure you clear it with whoever you did the job for, and if in doubt ask the other actor if they mind you using a clip with them in it.

I would like to market myself as a versatile voice actor. How can my reel reflect this, without boring my listener?

Generally speaking, my advice for voice artists trying to get into commercials is not to go too far with the versatility angle. Hundreds of people can do a bad American accent; most producers will hire an American voice artist if they want an American voice.

The variety in a commercial reel tends to come from the different types of approach you'll take to each script – it could be conversational, hard sell, seductive, blokey etc BUT it's still your natural voice that we're trying to sell with your reel. Anything you put on the reel has to be stuff you can do comfortably, and do well. If you get work

"Generally speaking, my advice for voice artists trying to get into commercials is not to go too far with the versatility angle"

from this (and that's the aim!) you need to be able to recreate everything you do on your reel at the drop of a hat if you get asked for it!

Should I experiment with different voices on my reel?

You certainly shouldn't be experimenting too much, no. If you're an impressionist for instance, and you want an impressions reel it will obviously contain plenty of different voices, but like the answer above - stick to your established, proven skills, experiment in your own time. For commercials I'd say definitely not. As a producer of showreels I've asked people to try out scripts or reads that they may not have thought of during the session, sometimes it works and sometimes it doesn't, but I'd never ask someone to try a different voice.

What will a sound engineer do to edit my work once I've left the studio?

The exact details of what the engineer will do depend on the type of reel and the material. Generally speaking, for commercials they would be cleaning up unwanted breaths and mouth noise, applying appropriate eq and compression and any other effects appropriate to the script, adding music and SFX where necessary, making sure the timing of the read is absolutely perfect and mixing all these elements together into a finished product. In short, everything they would normally do to produce a professional sounding piece of work!

How long should my voicereel be?

Again speaking specifically for commercials, many engineers will mix the six scripts (generally 20-30 secs each but they could be anywhere between 2- 60 sec if the script and the read justify it) plus narrative (between 30 and 1 minute 30) and also produce a 60-90 second montage edited together from all the best bits of the finished material. This is a lot punchier and more immediate than listening to all of your scripts one by one, and it's often these montages that you'll see on voice agency websites.

Tim O'Donoghue is a Sound Engineer at the award-winning Angell Sound studio in Soho. Angell Sound are leading specialists in audio post production for television, cinema, radio advertising and digital platforms. **www.angellsound.co.uk**

Voiceover Work

the voiceover gallery

THIS GUIDE WAS KINDLY WRITTEN BY JAMES BONALLACK, DIRECTOR OF THE VOICEOVER GALLERY

How can you succeed in the voiceover business? You've got a brand new voice showreel with a trendy mix of commercials, corporates and narratives and now you're ready to sit down behind the mic and start earning the big money. Let's start with the good news: if you're Jenny Eclair, Tom Baker or Jack Dee it's easy – your agent calls you, you turn up at the studio where people make a huge fuss of you, you voice a 30-second commercial and then when the cheque arrives you think there's one zero too many on the end. If not, much as with anything else in life, you'll get out what you put in – if you're lucky. Having a great voice is the easy bit – making money with it is a whole different story. This snapshot of the UK voiceover industry will help you make some informed decisions and perhaps avoid some painful mistakes.

Getting started is the most difficult part. People will not be beating a path to your door; you're going to have to get them interested in you and, more importantly, your voice and what you can do with it.

Three golden rules
A producer is looking for three things in a voice. First, that you have a voice that's worth paying for, which means that your voice will have certain qualities. It doesn't mean smooth or rich or sexy or hard sell or sporty or that your voice is recognisable. It doesn't mean that you can narrate or sightread effortlessly for hours. It doesn't even mean that you are studio savvy and know what the engineer wants before he does! It simply means that your voice has got a certain something that they - or their client - feels fits their requirements, which is why your reel has got you the phone call and you are nervously pacing down a Soho side street looking for a studio with a name like Beach (if they

think they're trendy) or Digital Sound and Video Mastering Ltd (if they don't care who thinks they're trendy).

The second thing the producer is expecting is that you do what it says on your demo or voiceover CV. That means if you say you narrate well then you had better be able to narrate well. If it says you're as cheap as chips because you've only done a bit of hospital radio before you decided to become a voice actor then their expectations will be very much less. The point is don't say you're a genius if you're not – you will be found out!

Finally, the third thing they want from you is that you can take direction. That simply means read what it says on the script, unless it's obviously not correct, listen to what you are being asked to do and do it without a fuss and to the best of your abilities. As you gain experience you'll develop confidence about voicing your opinions, but to begin with concentrate on getting the right result and showing willing.

A word about sound engineers. Studios are strange places populated by sound engineers who don't see much sunlight. But remember they are your friends. They make you sound good: they help you drop in just after where you inexplicably fluffed for the fifth time and their skills makes you come across as being better than you probably are. Learn the jargon and get a reputation for turning up early and being professional. These are the shortcuts to recommendations and repeat business. The same goes for producers and the money people who pay your invoices – network with anyone who might be useful!

Voiceover agents

One of the questions I hear most from new voices is 'How do you find a voiceover agent?'. Start by sending your demo to agents and anyone else who might be useful – but call first. There is virtually no chance that an agent will take you on if you send your demo in unsolicited. Your chances improve when you take the trouble to ask intelligent questions about their business and how you could be of use to them, supported by a clear voice CV and a short demo with your phone number on both the CD and on the box spine.

"An agency will be much more interested in you if you can bring some existing work with you and you are prepared to offer an exclusive deal"

Before you dive straight in and start making phone calls it's also worth really considering if you need an agent just yet. Agents are going to be a lot more interested in you if you've got some solid voicing experience under your belt before you start to pester them for representation. Whilst it's certainly true that a good agent will greatly improve your earnings and supply you with regular work, there are equally many voices languishing unused on agency books. I can think of one agency in particular which has 100 or more voices on its books. Their top people work regularly but the rest don't get a look in – the agent is too busy worrying about his star clients. Agencies do hire but only after developing relationships with voices they know. An agency will be much more interested in you if you can bring some existing work with you and you are prepared to offer them an exclusive deal, at least for your TV and advertising work.

Furthermore, with the advent of online voiceover portals many agencies are booking voices without actually going to the trouble of representing them. The relationship builds and eventually they slot into the agency by default.

(By the way that's a two way street. Many savvy voices are now representing themselves and are represented by more than one agent to find as many outlets as possible for their voice. Having said that, the traditional model of putting all your work via one agent is under threat but still very much in place at the top of the food chain. If you have a top agent you won't want to upset them by touting for work outside of that relationship.)

Internet portals

If you're at all familiar with voiceover portals you'll instantly see the advantages. You're on the internet 24/7; you have your own URL (web address) without having to set up your own site; you can be searched by producers in various ways and you can take advantage of other online databases to send your link to potential clients. The better portals will also offer free advice and information about aspects of the industry and directories of relevant contacts.

As you develop your skills and find you have a good client base you might want to think about setting up a home studio, perhaps even with an ISDN capability. This is particularly useful for voices that do a lot of radio spots or who live outside London. The advantages are that you are more competitive and can save the production company time by editing your own .wav files. This makes using you convenient and in all probability very good value. The disadvantage is that you could find yourself very isolated as the business is very much one of networking in the pub after the session. For more on the pros and cons of home studios have a look at www.myvoicestudio.co.uk.

Here it is in a nutshell: be proactive and be professional. The industry is very competitive and luck and timing play a big part.

The Voiceover Gallery is a specialist London voice over agency with voice over studios in London and Manchester.
www.thevoiceovergallery.co.uk

How I Became a Character Voice Artist

A Q&A WITH CAMERON BAIRD

© John Nichols

Could you introduce us to a few of your characters? How did they come about?
While at school I created a voice character called Josephine. She is about 89 and she came about by playing with what voice artists now call voice placement. Josephine's voice is placed in the front of the mouth and her voice can only be done by creating a half moon caricature unhappy face.

That's interesting! Could you tell us a little more about how you place your different voices?
I learnt that when trying to impersonate cartoon voices like Kermit the Frog, the voice could be placed anywhere in the mouth. I found that to impersonate Kermit the Frog, I had to move the sound to the back of my throat and I would do a short 'erm' sound to start the impression.

Another character I created later on was called Gerald. I'm unsure exactly when I came up with Gerald but again his voice was created by facial expressions and movements in the jaw. Both Josephine and Gerald are very old and I did think of creating an animation about both of them, voicing both characters myself. That hasn't happened yet, but I still try to improve both characters and I don't think I will stop developing them.

Could you tell us a little about the process of recording cartoons?
Sometimes the client might give you a description of what the character is like and an accent, for instance: A rat with a cheeky side to him, American accent. At other times you can get a script with a picture of the animation character, and the script might have character information.

It might be worth auditioning for more than one character or saying in your cover letter to the company, I hope you don't mind but I've also attached another character I would like to play.

Exploring your voice and keeping it flexible is very important for animation work, so working on any age of character is important.

What advice would you give to actors who are starting out?
From what I have learnt so far, my tips and advice for actors starting out would be:

- Believe in yourself and have confidence that you will do a great job. A casting director may well have made their minds up in the first few seconds [of an audition]. So just go for it!

- Keep vocal exercises up and practice everyday, remembering the techniques and exercises you have been taught.

- Keep going to auditions or auditioning for voiceovers and don't give up.

- If you do intend on doing voiceover work as a professional career it is worth researching about home studios as it can cost quite a lot to go into studios. I have my own small home studio for recording voice, but as I am also a singer and songwriter I also use it to record my songs. My current set up is my PC with Mixcraft 6, Focusrite Saffire Pro 14 and a Rode NT1-A Microphone – which I personally think is the best microphone for recording voice. I also have an Editors Keys Portable Vocal Booth.

"If you do intend on doing voiceover work as a professional career it is worth researching about home studios as it can cost quite a lot to go into studios"

In my experience, it also helps to read books which explain about how the voice works and how you can achieve different objectives. I recommend *The Actor Speaks* by Patsy Rodenburg, *Voice-Overs – A Practical Guide* by Bernard Graham Shaw, *Speaking Shakespeare* by Patsy Rodenburg. If you are interested in voiceover for animation, I suggest getting the book *Voice-Over for Animation* by Jean Ann Wright and M J Lallo.

What's the best advice you've heard?

Do your best, you can't do any better than that. Just go for it!

*Cameron Baird is an actor, voiceover artist and singer / songwriter and currently has a single called Red Petals on iTunes written by Cameron Baird and Henry Askew. His website is **www.cameron-baird.com**.*

Online Casting Services

Despite some very old traditions, the world of acting has fully embraced the power of the web. No longer do casting directors and agents have to store folders full of paper CVs and headshots, using the web they have access to thousands of actors' CVs at the push of a button and last-minute jobs can be cast in hours.

With the use of powerful search engines, they also now have the ability to find actors of any ethnicity, age, size, shape and language, quickly and easily. The use of showreels and voicereels has become increasingly important as casting directors and agents can use this to shortlist actors instead of spending copious amounts of time and money inviting actors to casting sessions.

Online casting services have also taken massive strides at breaking down the exclusivity of the acting industry. Roles and casting details can now be shared and communicated on the web to actors from all across the UK. For actors wishing to take control of their career, online casting services can be a godsend. Where traditionally it was difficult to find out about castings if you didn't have agency representation, you can now submit yourself for roles.

An online casting service is probably the most important tool for any actor intending to make a successful career. The main use of the online service is to find and apply for work, to find an agent, to network and to promote yourself.

Similar to the rules regarding headshots, showreels and agent applications, creating an excellent online profile comes with its own do's and don'ts. Here are our Top Tips for making the most out of our service:

1. First impressions still count
Being online gives you access to the world from your living room sofa. There is nothing more satisfying than sitting in your pyjamas with your bowl of cereal and being able to apply for a top casting but always

"An online casting service is probably the most important tool for any actor intending to make a successful career"

remember you are not 100% free from judgement. We remain a vain bunch and first impressions do still count. Instead of the focus being on you, the attention turns to your online profile. So make sure it is crisp and clean. The biggest turn offs for casting directors are an out of date or half complete profile, which give the impression of a lack of interest and commitment. A poor profile can do more damage than not having one at all. If you are going to have a profile online, make sure you are committed to maintaining it!

2. Be interesting and busy

All sites will allow you to write a section 'About You'. This is your chance to introduce yourself as a person and it's the part of your profile where you can be creative and write something interesting. It should be engaging, informative and coherent and should tell people what you do well and what you want to do more of in the future. Things to include can be current role, background, experiences and any additional skills that make you stand out. However, do not waffle: one or two paragraphs are sufficient.

3. Be contactable

There is quite often the debate about how much information you put on the internet, but the whole point of an online profile is to let people know who you are and how to contact you. At Casting Call Pro we see some of our best castings come through as urgent requirements. The internet is fast, but a telephone call is still quicker. Casting directors in a hurry are not willing to send an email and wait - they will look for a profile with a telephone number and make the call. As a security measure, at CCP we only give employers access to these details, but we still see so many profiles missing a telephone number - and hence missing some great opportunities.

4. Be literate

In a time when an average casting gets hundreds of strong applicants, the casting director is looking for any little excuse to help whittle the numbers down to a shortlist. Bad spelling and grammar is a sure fire way of excluding yourself from the running. No excuses - get it right!

5. Be professional

With great power comes great responsibility. Remember you are being watched at all times online. CCP, personal websites, Facebook, Twitter, Linkedin all give casting directors access to your history. If you want to blow off some steam or rant and rave, do it over a drink with your friends. Don't publish it on the web. A new trend is for professionals to separate their professional presence online from their personal one i.e. creating an open access web page, Facebook page and Twitter account to promote their professional activities to the world, but also maintaining a separate personal online presence accessible by only a very selective group of friends!

Being online is a great way of getting your foot through the door and has completely changed the way the industry works, giving people transparency and access to jobs across the globe. But remember, it will never replace the impact you have from an actual face to face meeting or a good hearty handshake

A-Z of Photographers

Quality, cost and style can vary enormously from one photographer to another, and a good photographer may well cost in excess of £250 for a session (and don't forget to check if they're VAT registered) so do your research before you invest. Most photographers have websites on which you can find out more about their services and costs, and browse examples of their work. It may sound expensive, but it really does pay dividends to have your headshots done properly. Some photographers offer discounts to students, recent graduates or Casting Call Pro members so always check before you book.

If you're considering a photography studio, ask which photographer you'll be working with and ask to see examples of their work. Taking an actor's headshot is a specific skill and a very specific style entirely different from modelling shots or wedding photography, so make sure your photographer knows what's involved to make sure you end up with the right product.

Before booking make sure you know how many shots the photographer will take, how long the shoot is and how many final images and/or prints are included in the price. If you get given digital images, make sure you're also provided with internet friendly files that can easily be emailed or uploaded to websites. If you're not confident with these technicalities, ask the photographer for more information. The photographer will own the rights to any of the photos they take of you and should also be credited whenever you display or print the picture: this is a legal obligation.

When choosing your photographer, word of mouth recommendation from fellow actors can be invaluable. Overleaf is a list of the Top 25 Most Popular Headshot Providers on Casting Call Pro. You can also check out our complete Photographer Directory via **www.casting-callpro.com/uk/psearch.php**

AM-LONDON
London
www.am-london.com
CCP CLIENTS: 185

BRANDON BISHOP PHOTOGRAPHY LTD
London
www.brandonbishopphotography.com
CCP CLIENTS: 488

CARL PROCTOR PHOTOGRAPHY
London
www.carlproctor.com/photos
CCP CLIENTS: 379

CAROLINE WEBSTER PHOTOGRAPHY
London
www.carolinewebster.co.uk
CCP CLIENTS: 215

CLAIRE GROGAN PHOTOGRAPHY
London
www.clairegrogan.co.uk
CCP CLIENTS: 748

FATIMAH NAMDAR
London
www.fatimahnamdar.dphoto.com
CCP CLIENTS: 330

FAYE THOMAS
London
www.fayethomas.com
CCP CLIENTS: 500

GEMMA MOUNT PHOTOGRAPHY
London
www.gemmamountphotography.com
CCP CLIENTS: 242

JENNIE SCOTT PHOTOGRAPHY
London
www.castingcallpro.com/uk/view.php?uid=312692
CCP CLIENTS: 264

JOHN CLARK PHOTOGRAPHY
London
www.johnclarkphotography.com
CCP CLIENTS: 1557

JOHN NICHOLS STUDIO
Manchester
www.johnnichols.co.uk
CCP CLIENTS: 551

KIRILL PHOTOGRAPHY
London
www.kirill.co.uk
CCP CLIENTS: 473

LB PHOTOGRAPHY
Redhill
www.lisabowerman.com/?page_id=26
CCP CLIENTS: 368

M.A.D PHOTOGRAPHY
London
www.mad-photography.co.uk
CCP CLIENTS: 909

MAGNUS HASTINGS
London
www.magnushastings.co.uk
CCP CLIENTS: 233

MICHAEL POLLARD
Manchester
www.michaelpollard.co.uk
CCP CLIENTS: 659

MICHAEL WHARLEY
London
www.michaelwharley.com
CCP CLIENTS: 196

NATASHA MERCHANT
London
www.natashamerchant.com
CCP CLIENTS: 257

NICHOLAS DAWKES PHOTOGRAPHY
London
www.nicholasdawkesphotography.co.uk
CCP CLIENTS: 475

PAUL BARRASS PHOTOGRAPHY
London
www.paulbarrass.co.uk
CCP CLIENTS: 197

PETE BARTLETT PHOTOGRAPHY
London
www.petebartlettheadshots.co.uk
CCP CLIENTS: 411

PETER SIMPKIN
London
www.petersimpkin.co.uk
CCP CLIENTS: 623

REMY HUNTER PHOTOGRAPHY
London
www.remyhunterphotography.com
CCP CLIENTS: 191

SHAMBHALA
London
www.castingcallpro.com/uk/view.php?uid=69007
CCP CLIENTS: 203

SHEILA BURNETT
London
www.sheilaburnett-photography.com
CCP CLIENTS: 281

SIMON ANNAND
London
www.simonannand.com
CCP CLIENTS: 175

STEVE LAWTON PHOTOGRAPHY
London
www.stevelawton.com
CCP CLIENTS: 389

VINCENT ABBEY PHOTOGRAPHY
South Manchester
www.vincentabbey.co.uk
CCP CLIENTS: 175

WOLF MARLOH
London
www.wolfmarloh.com
CCP CLIENTS: 398

A-Z of Showreel Providers

These days, with easy-to-use movie-making software widely available, it can be tempting to put together a showreel yourself, or to ask a tech-handy friend to do it for you. As with headshots, there is a huge amount of skill and expertise involved in putting together a good quality showreel and a poorly edited video that looks like it was cobbled together is not going to do you any favours. You're a business and you need to invest in good tools at the outset to put yourself in the best possible position to book jobs. As such it really is worth going to the expense of using a professional company who specialise in showreels for actors.

Given that the costs for producing a showreel are high it's essential that you choose a company with a good track record of working with actors, so that the end results present you in the best possible way. Once again, ask around for recommendations from other actors and always do your research on a company before parting with any cash: look at samples of their work and check prices on the website. The following is a list of The 30 Showreel Providers used most regularly by Casting Call Pro members. You can also see our complete Showreel Provider Directory at **www.castingcallpro.com/uk/showreelsearch.php**

2B-SCENE
Lancashire
www.2b-scene.co.uk
CCP CLIENTS: 28

ACTORS APPAREL
London
www.actorsapparel.com
CCP CLIENTS: 15

ACTOR SHOWREELS
London
www.actorshowreels.co.uk
CCP CLIENTS: 36

THE ACTOR'S ONE-STOP SHOP
London
www.actorsonestopshop.com
CCP CLIENTS: 468

ACTORSHOP
London
www.actorshop.co.uk
CCP CLIENTS: 14

BIRMINGHAM SHOWREELS
Birmingham
www.birminghamshowreels.co.uk
CCP CLIENTS: 9

BRIAN BARNES SHOWREEL SERVICES
London
www.osmiumfilms.co.uk/briansreels/Showreels.html
CCP CLIENTS: 4

FREEZEFRAME PRODUCTIONS
Preston
www.freezeframeproductions.co.uk/actors-showreels
CCP CLIENTS: 7

HI FILMS TV
North Yorkshire
www.hifilms.wordpress.com/contact
CCP CLIENTS: 14

MACHEATH PRODUCTIONS
London
www.thealchemyofscreenacting.co.uk/115_Home.asp
CCP CLIENTS: 48

MARK KEMPNER
Cheltenham
www.markkempner.co.uk
CCP CLIENTS: 23

MICKSING PRODUCTIONS
London
www.micksingproductions.com
CCP CLIENTS: 10

NOVEMBER FILMS
London
http://www.novemberfilms.co.uk
CCP CLIENTS: 7

PELINOR
London
www.pelinor.com

CCP CLIENTS: 54

THE REEL DEAL SHOWREEL CO
Surrey
www.thereel-deal.co.uk
CCP CLIENTS: 61

THE REEL GEEKS
London
www.thereelgeeks.com
CCP CLIENTS: 10

RETRO REELS
London
www.retroreels.co.uk
CCP CLIENTS: 15

ROUND ISLAND
London
www.roundisland.net
CCP CLIENTS: 169

SHOWREELS4U
Herts
www.showreels4u.blogspot.co.uk
CCP CLIENTS: 21

SHOWREEL EDITS
London
www.facebook.com/showreelediting
CCP CLIENTS: 8

THE SHOWREEL SHOP
London
www.showreel-shop.com
CCP CLIENTS: 8

SHOWREELZ
London
www.showreelz.com
CCP CLIENTS: 30

SLICK SHOWREELS
London
www.slickshowreels.co.uk
CCP CLIENTS: 12

SMALL SCREEN SHOWREELS
London
www.smallscreenshowreels.co.uk
CCP CLIENTS: 13

SONICPOND STUDIO
London
www.sonicpond.co.uk
CCP CLIENTS: 26

STOP & PLAY
London
www.smallscreenshowreels.co.uk
CCP CLIENTS: 13

TAKE FIVE STUDIO
London
www.takefivestudio.com
CCP CLIENTS: 8

TWITCH FILMS
London
www.twitchfilms.co.uk
CCP CLIENTS: 42

VINCENT ABBEY PHOTOGRAPHY
South Manchester
www.vincentabbey.co.uk
CCP CLIENTS: 8

VISUAL CLOUD MEDIA
Manchester
www.visualcloudmedia.com
CCP CLIENTS: 7

A-Z of Voicereel Providers

As with headshots and showreels, investing in a professionally produced voicereel can really pay dividends. The following is a list of The 30 Voicereel Providers used most regularly by Casting Call Pro members. You can also see our complete Voicereel Provider Directory at **www.castingcallpro.com/uk/voicereelsearch.php**

THE ACTOR'S ONE-STOP SHOP
London
www.actorsonestopshop.com
CCP CLIENTS: 7

BRIAN BARNES SHOWREEL SERVICES
London
www.osmiumfilms.co.uk/briansreels/Showreels.html
CCP CLIENTS: 4

CRYING OUT LOUD PRODUCTIONS
London
www.cryingoutloud.co.uk
CCP CLIENTS: 368

CUT GLASS PRODUCTIONS
Dorset
www.cutglassproductions.com
CCP CLIENTS: 238

DAVID ANGUS AUDIO
Somerset
www.castingcallpro.com/uk/view.php?uid=164889
CCP CLIENTS: 44

HATS OFF STUDIOS
Oxfordshire
www.hatsoffstudios.com
CCP CLIENTS: 13

HOTREELS
London
www.hotreels.co.uk
CCP MEMBERS: 8

PACIFIC AUDIO
Glasgow
www.pacificaudio.co.uk
CCP CLIENTS: 23

ROUND ISLAND
London
www.roundisland.net
CCP CLIENTS: 93

THE SHOWREEL LTD
London
www.theshowreel.com
CCP CLIENTS: 88

SHOWREELZ
London
www.showreelz.com
CCP CLIENTS: 8

SILVER-TONGUED PRODUCTIONS
Sidcup
www.silver-tongued.co.uk
CCP CLIENTS: 55

SONICPOND STUDIO
London
www.sonicpond.co.uk
CCP CLIENTS: 186

SOUNDS WILDE
London
www.soundswilde.com
CCP CLIENTS: 19

SOUNDTRACKS STUDIOS
London
www.soundtracks.co.uk
CCP CLIENTS: 4

SUGAR POD PRODUCTIONS
London
www.sugarpodproductions.com
CCP CLIENTS: 15

VOICE4HIRE CREATIVE
London
www.voice4hire.tv
CCP CLIENTS: 4

VOICEOVER SOHO
London
www.sohovoices.co.uk
CCP CLIENTS: 53

VOICEREELS.CO.UK
London
www.voicereels.co.uk
CCP CLIENTS: 63

WIRELESS THEATRE VOICE-REELS
London
www.wirelesstheatrecompany.co.uk/index.php
/wireless-theatre-voicereels
CCP MEMBERS: 11

Find your voice with
VOICEOVERSOHO

Every voice is unique and needs to be considered individually to highlight particular talents and abilities.

£299 - COMPLETE VOICE-REEL
10 scripts individually tailored, recorded and mixed with music and sound effects in three 90 minute sessions.

£99 - VOICE-REEL STARTER
3 scripts recorded and mixed with music and sound effects in 1 hour.

"A good voice-reel books you jobs & with Voiceover Soho I got exactly that."
- *Omri Rose*

"Voiceover Soho got me where I am - recording video games to commercials!!!"
- *Fiona Rene*

"Great experience, professional & down to earth. Soon after, the work began to come in. I really owe you guys a lot!"
- *Thomas Arnold*

"Even established voice-overs need shaking up! Having worked with Voiceover Soho many times in my career, I had no hesitation in placing myself in their hands. They did me proud."
- *Trish Bertram*

For more information visit voiceoversoho.co.uk

0207 437 3202
info@voiceoversoho.co.uk
@voiceoversoho

VOICEOVER SOHO

Abel & Cole

Are you an outgoing, charming, actorly type? Thought so.

Fancy selling fruit and veg at the door (great pay and no hard sell)?

Join our team of part time workers earning great money and help Abel & Cole conquer the world of organic vegetables! This great business is looking for friendly, enthusiastic and self employed brilliant people to sell fruit and veg subscriptions.

Excellent commission and staff discount. Training provided. £40–£100 per shift (10.00am – 2.00pm/4.30pm - 8.00pm) for those achieving targets plus travel expenses paid. No hard sell!

Please email an up to date CV and a short and snappy introduction about yourself and why you think you'd be suited to this role to:

jobs@abelandcole.co.uk or call 020 8944 3769

Providing flexible, 'day-job' employment to actors for over 20 years...

RSVP is an electric & vibrant call centre like no other!

The difference? - All our staff are actors!

Time off for auditions & a working environment to answer all your prayers!

Full time, flexible work on inbound & outbound campaigns – sales & customer service, offering great rates of pay

With over 20 years' experience in employing performers, we understand your real career comes first!

Come join the fun!

t - 020 7536 3548   e - jobs@rsvp.co.uk

www.rsvp.co.uk

@RSVPCallCentres

EMMA BULLIVANT PHOTOGRAPHY©

www.emmabullivant.com / emmabullivant@me.com / eb_img TWITTER :-)

www.EMMABULLIVANT.COM

Your showreel is crucial

So make it with a director who
can ensure you deliver your best

Nick Reed will help you select scenes and
fully prep your performance

Scenes will be recorded to HD or 2K with separate sound

Your scenes will be edited and combined to produce a high
quality reel that is engaging and unique

For more information, sample reels and testimonials
visit www.nickreed.net

- Teaches TV and Film from day one

- Offers a 15 month Postgraduate course in
Acting - MA and Diploma Level 5

- One year Foundation course in Acting

- Three year Acting course - BA Hons and
Diploma Level 6

- Two year Stage Management and
Technical Theatre course

THE STAGE 100
A W A R D S
SCHOOL OF THE YEAR 2013

For further information on any of our
courses please email info@alra.co.uk
or call 020 8870 6475

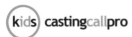

Chapter 4
Life as an Actor

An Interview with... Zoë Wanamaker

© Paul Grover

Zoë Wanamaker is one of the UK's most respected actors. In a career spanning over forty years she has worked prolifically in film, theatre and television. Zoë's parents (American actor / director Sam Wanamaker and Charlotte Holland, also an actor) moved the family to London from the US in 1952, when Zoë was three years old. A prominent liberal, Sam Wanamaker was blacklisted during the era of the McCarthy trials. Transplanted to London, the Wanamakers made a life in the UK, with Sam zealously championing and overseeing the reconstruction of Shakespeare's Globe Theatre, which since 1997 has stood proudly on the South Bank. In 1970, after studying for three years at the Central School of Speech and Drama, Zoë immediately began her professional acting career. Her television work includes Edge of Darkness, Doctor Who, Love Hurts, and the long-running successful sitcom My Family. Film credits include Wilde, and Harry Potter and the Philosopher's Stone. Zoë's theatre work is extensive (a full list would run the length of this book!), with some of the many highlights being Mother Courage and Her Children, Electra, All My Sons, and The Cherry Orchard. Winner of numerous awards, including two Olivier Awards for Best Actress, nominee for many more, including BAFTAs and Tonys, and, since 2000, a Commander of the British Empire (CBE), Zoë lives in North London.

On a crisp Autumn morning Simon Dale from Casting Call Pro was welcomed into her home where he was met with fresh coffee and freewheeling conversation – candid reflections upon Zoë's career to date, and what it is to be an actor.

(The interview was a patchwork of questions, responses, thoughts, and sideways segues... so what follows is a threading together of questions and answers to form a loose narrative.)

When did you know you wanted to be an actor, and what do you think influenced your becoming an actor?
From the beginning we [Zoë and her two sisters] were very much exposed to the arts. With my parents being actors themselves and this country being a refuge and being American we went to concerts, the theatre... My parents explored the country they had brought us to and we were given every opportunity to see things... [Pause.] When my father went to play Iago at Stratford, when I was about ten years old, there was a very visceral moment... staying in a big house on the River Avon... my father used to row to the theatre!... the romanticism of Stratford... that's probably where I remember acting playing a big part in my life. I remember going back stage and the smell of grease paint, the costumes, and the transformation of people turning into characters. It was the romanticism and the freedom that caught my imagination. I wanted to be part of that world of play and fantasy. It was the play of it all and the romance that drew me to it...

[Zoë went on to say, later in the interview, that while that was her experience, she knows many successful actors with entirely different backgrounds, with no overt exposure to the arts and the world of acting, who were drawn to, and seized by, the passion for acting.]

It was in me to act. It either is or it isn't. And I was lucky enough to be surrounded by the arts and people and influences that my parents introduced us to.

Did you find training useful, and do you think it is essential?
It's a hard question as it's very personal. I can only say that at that time, for me, training was a very good thing. Now, of course, it's not so easy to get into drama school because the profession is so overcrowded. There are so many different courses out there... Different schools have different ways of working and teaching...

[Zoë mentions that Central now offer a puppetry course, something that was unheard of in her day, and that the range of courses and specialism on offer is now much greater.]

"You have to find the drama school that fits your soul – which is difficult when you're beginning to find out who you are"

You have to find the drama school that fits your soul – which is difficult when you're beginning to find out who you are... Training did prepare me for stage work... you have to go to the very basics of what it is to be an actor... walking and talking! [Zoe chuckles at the seeming simplicity of it, while conveying that the process of learning and discovery is anything but simple.] You learn how to walk and talk! It sounds easier than it is. It's difficult because we're so physically bound in ourselves... my dad used to say that 'an actor has to be a juggler, a dancer, a swordsman, a mime artist... to be able to swim, to walk, to talk, to be flexible and to be ready'. As an actor you have to be everybody potentially you could be... and, for me, training helped discover how to approach a character and a text... I know a lot of actors who did a first degree in English Literature and they had more of an academic viewpoint... [which is where choosing your course comes in]. You also learn to look around you, at your fellow human beings and fellow actors, and you realise the kaleidoscopic views there are out there, and all the different ways of playing a character.

The problem is that if you do it [begin an acting career without any training] and you get paid for it, it can be very seductive – why would you go to drama school and be taught what you think you know instinctively?

But if you're not sure about who you are and where you fit, training can give you a great grounding. [Zoë takes a sip of coffee.] Of course when you get out there you find that there's no work!

Do you still have to audition for theatre parts?

Not in this country. For film, yes, for TV it depends. I didn't have to audition for My Family. [On auditioning for film.] In America it's very different. Unless you're extremely famous in filmic terms you have to audition in America. And there the process is very different. You walk into a room with about forty people, casting directors, casting directors' assistants, assistants' assistants, financiers, producers... it's a very different experience... I auditioned for Harry Potter. I did have a script but I didn't learn it – and they don't like that! [Laughter.]

How do you cope with rejection?

You don't. Sometimes I understand. It helped that before I went to drama school I worked for a casting director. It nearly put me off for life! I found it shocking and scary, but I do understand that when someone walks into a room half a judgement has been made already about whether you're right for the particular part – and it's an understanding of all the other chemical elements that come together in a production – if you can understand that there are all the different elements, the look of everything, the feel of everything that the director has as their vision then to some extent you can take a certain amount of rejection.

[Simon mentions that he knows actors who have been for auditions, not got the part, and have then been contacted months later by the casting director offering them an audition for a completely different part.]

Absolutely. And you have to be strong, you have to have a carapace. You have to be protected by your own self-belief. The problem is actors don't always have that, but you do have a passion, a passion which has to be channelled. Auditions are supposed to be a channel, but I'm not good at auditions, I never have been. I don't like to do things out of context. But that's me. It's never wrong to audition, it's all about finding what fits into the jigsaw puzzle, if you fit.

Have you ever come away from a role and felt utterly happy with it, and what do you think does it take for a role to 'click'?
No, I don't think I've ever been totally happy with a role. There is always room for improvement. I think for me the most fulfilling role was playing Kattrin in Mother Courage and her Children with Judi Dench at The Barbican, a Howard Davies production. Kattrin has no lines, she's mute, but I felt that I could explore physical movement with intention. With the research that I did beforehand and within the production, the character of Kattrin and that particular production were very important to me. I was using my body as a form of expression within a theatrical piece, a difficult piece. Electra was also very satisfying. That was a very good experience, and going to New York with it was wonderful. [Zoe was nominated for a Tony for her performance in Electra.] That was a character that at the time I felt completely, understandably, with – she appeared completely instinctively and in fact had to be put into a box on a nightly basis. I had to make a conscious effort to get rid of her after a show. That's the first time that had ever happened to me. She did have to be put away.

Conversely, there must have been nights in your theatrical career when, for whatever reason, the audience is muted and only dead air is coming back at you... how do you cope?
You feel like a swan not being able to take off, paddling but not getting anywhere! You can't take off and that ruins your concentration but of course you have to get through it and get to the end.

What is it then that makes a character and a performance come together?
It's a freedom on stage, while having control. It's when you see a performance where you as the audience feel comfortable, you don't feel uneasy for the actor.

Does that come later in a run? Do you get progressively better?
I hope so. Initially one is frightened, you want that feeling that the audience can relax and you can relax, what I call 'hovercrafting' – lifting and raising yourself above the stage. You are it [the character], and it is you. That's what I try and work on throughout a run and it

gets easier as you are playing and getting to know the character in front of an audience. In rehearsals you're struggling with lines, understanding the text, taking direction, how do I feel at this point, and so on? Once you start to achieve that freedom, in front of an audience... it's indescribable. And that's when you start to progress. Eight shows a week [as is usual for a theatrical run with matinees, and it was for the much acclaimed production of All My Sons which played in London's West End in 2010-11] is a workout. Once you have that freedom you play with it, you improve it. In contrast, a break in a production schedule can make it difficult to recover that work in progress... for me – it breaks the concentration, the rhythm of the exploration, that freedom that the character and the story demands... I find that discombobulating!

Do you read your own reviews?
I stopped reading my reviews when I did The Importance of Being Earnest at the National – a bad review crippled me for the rest of the run. It's not worth it. Your self-belief, my self-belief, was so fragile that it scuppered me. I think ninety-nine percent of the actors I know don't read their reviews. It's not like being a mathematician where you can get a number wrong... to have one person make that judgement... it's subjective. If you're insecure about something then it's not good, it's not helpful to one's ego, and that's what we, the actor, has to protect. [Simon: And I suppose that doesn't change, no matter how many productions you've done?] That's right. It never changes.

Does the public perception that acting is easy, that anybody could do it, irritate you? Do you think that misconception that acting is easy still exists? And how do you view the cult of celebrity?
It saddens me because in every other European country and in America there is a greater, deeper respect for actors. In this country

"I think ninety-nine percent of the actors I know don't read their reviews"

there is an old-fashioned, creaky sexism about it as well, with actresses synonymous with old Vaudeville performers with the feather boas and lipstick. The respect [here, in the UK] for actors and the work they do isn't what it is in other countries. It is a profession, it is a craft. It takes work. [Simon: but then you're called a luvvie.] Exactly. I hate that word! It's difficult to describe acting – you sound pretentious and self-indulgent [chuckle] but then that's what it is to some extent.

[On the rise of celebrity culture and the fad of fame.] It intrigues me. It's obvious that budgets are being cut, that drama is being cut, the common denominator has diminished and good drama and good writing is having to fight for its life.... But we could say that about the whole of society... what's happening in the world of acting is a reflection of wider society – and performers, writers, artists, have to reflect society... but we mustn't lose the heritage which has been handed down and which is so rich, and that's why theatre is so important – and while it only preaches to a small minority of people, that small minority are, to some extent, the fabric of our society. In that sense it [celebrity, the fame-followers] doesn't depress me, it fires me up to struggle against it.

[Discussing the changing nature of viewing habits and the way television is commissioned.]

The second television series I did was Love Hurts, the first Paradise Postponed. Then we would get fourteen or fifteen million viewers, the same with My Family. Since then television viewing numbers and habits have changed dramatically. There are now so many more channels, and the way we watch television has changed... In America you sign yourself for a three or seven year contract. In this country they don't do that, we didn't know if the series [My Family] would be re-commissioned from one year to the next.

[Simon asked about the differences in acting for theatre and television.]

Television allows the actor to be more 'in your face'. I never got as many voiceovers as when I was in Love Hurts. Television gives you exposure – it's salesmanship. It [high profile television roles] changed my life to some extent. People recognised me in the street and it led to other work, but I always wanted to, and tried to, work in theatre after a television series. Every time I finished a series I would try and do a play. As an actor I want to be able to do as many different things as I can. One would like to be able to be a chameleon, trying different mediums as much as you can, learning about oneself and one's parameters, strengths and weakness. What one can get better at. You never stop learning.

Acting is a difficult and very competitive profession. What advice would you give to actors just starting out?
Of my year at drama school I think two or three that I know of have remained in the business. That's out of twenty or twenty-five people. [Pause.] There have been times when I haven't worked and it's very difficult to hold on to your self belief. You have to give yourself another string to your bow, something that keeps your ego intact, so that to some extent you feel you are doing something instead of sitting at home feeling angry and miserable and resentful. You have to keep your love of life up and that's the most important thing. Find another thing that you love and that excites you, and allows you to put a roof over your head and enjoy yourself and who you are. And, being an actor, go to shows, go to galleries, listen to music, watch television – whatever it is that excites and stimulates you... see what's going on and absorb as much as you can because that comes out when you're acting.... Because, and it's back to the beginning, as an actor you have to be everybody potentially you could be.

A very grateful thank you to Zoë for her honesty and grace in being interviewed for Actors' Handbook, for her lovely coffee and delightful company. We wish her well in the next chapter in her rich and varied career.

Auditions & Applying for Work

Casting Directors

Casting directors are employed by directors and producers to sieve through the pool of acting talent and suggest the most appropriate actors for a part. Armed with a character breakdown and an encyclopaedic knowledge of actors, they'll shortlist suitable candidates who they think will match the role's requirements and the director's expectations.

Casting directors tend to be brought in for specific projects. There are more than 250 casting directors in the UK, some working as individual freelancers, some as part of an in-house department in larger theatres, and others as part of larger companies or collectives.

In many cases the casting director does not have the final say over who gets a role – this is usually the decision of the director and producer. It's important to remember the casting director is on the side of the actor – good vision and choices reflect well on them and their reputation will be consolidated by a successful casting. It's in their interest for you to get the job just as much as it is yours!

Q&A with Casting Director
Benjamin Newsome

BENJAMIN NEWSOME IS A CASTING DIRECTOR WHO WORKS ACROSS THEATRE, FILM AND ONLINE PRODUCTIONS. HIS NUMEROUS THEATRE CREDITS INCLUDE THE MYSTERY OF EDWIN DROOD (THE ARTS THEATRE), SEARCH FOR A TWITTER STAR (THE LYRIC THEATRE), I DO! I DO! (RIVERSIDE STUDIOS), CRAZY FOR YOU THE MUSICAL (UPSTAIRS AT THE GATEHOUSE), THE MARK OF LIA (THE BROCKLEY JACK), POP FACTOR (UK TOUR), OLD GOAT SONG (THE LION & UNICORN) AND THE BOY WHO WAS WOODY ALLEN (THE PLEASANCE). FILM CREDITS INCLUDE NEIL AND POST IT, WITH NEW FEATURE FILM DISORIENTATED TO HIT SCREENS 2015.

(side text) © Nick Butcher

Q. What sort of content should actors include in their covering letter?

Short, sweet & simple is the key. Name, contact details, the production you're applying for and the role. Always nice to throw a little extra in there as well, for example, if the role you're applying for needs an actor-musician then mentioning that you're Grade 8 Piano will help.

Q. Are there common mistakes actors make when applying for roles?

YES! Read the role correctly! So many actors just read the first part like the age and ethnicity and miss the vocal range / quality or the height requirements. If a casting director brings you in thinking that you fit the role requirements and you don't, then it makes the casting director look bad and they'll remember you for the wrong reasons. Always know your strengths: there's no point in applying for the role of a dancer if you're not a strong dancer. So many performers are disillusioned about what they think they can do. Know yourself, your strengths and, most importantly, your weaknesses as the industry is not the place to work on them: class and college is the place to do that.

Q. When it comes to headshots, do you like to see an image that relates directly to a role (eg, geeky, tough guy etc)? And do you have a preference between colour or black and white shots?

When casting musical theatre it's not that important to have a headshot specific to the role. Though, of course, if you're casting High School Musical it wouldn't hurt to send your smiley headshots. For

"Just because you've been signed by an agent, you should NEVER leave your life in one person's hands!"

TV / Film castings in my opinion it's important to have a variety of headshots that show you with different looks. For example if you're casting a period drama then a headshot with your hair tied back would work well, or for example if I'm casting a homeless person then a headshot with a beard could help swing that audition slot. For the money you pay for headshots nowadays you might as well get your money's worth and get lots of different images: don't waste all your cash on buying the same pretty photo five times. One thing that does really get to me: research your photographers. A lot of the time the ones that make people look beautiful are not the best photographers for the industry as you walk into your audition looking nothing like your headshot. They need to look like you: a headshot is for the industry, NOT to give your gran to put on her fireplace.

I personally have no preference towards B&W or colour. The fashion of 2013 seems to be outside shots in natural light.

Q. What do you think is the optimum length and/or format for a showreel? In other words, how long until you stop watching?!
The longest is 2 minutes without a doubt! I usually stop watching at 60 seconds or fast forward through it. Keep it simple, it doesn't have to be all expensive and flashy. It's nice to include a few headshots or portfolio images in between scenes.

Q. How do you feel about actors making general contact? Or should they only contact you regarding a specific production?
I'm 100% for it. Just because you've been signed by an agent, you should NEVER leave your life in one person's hands! That one person is also looking after another 50-100 people, so always do things for

yourself. It's more helpful to be contacted for specific productions and specific roles.

Q. Do you attend graduate showcases or productions? What are the factors that help you decide which ones to attend?

Yes, as many as possible. The feeling of July arriving with 6000 new graduates entering the industry gives me sleepless nights! Your showcase HAS to be in Central London: it's just not right to make a casting director travel out of London, and it rarely happens due to the time and expense involved.

Q. Are you also happy to attend performances or productions to see an actor's work? If so, how should they invite you and how much notice should they give?

I'm always happy to attend any production. Maybe not if you're ensemble or not featured a lot. You should NEVER expect a Casting Director to pay, as we are actually working whilst at the production - who would pay to do work!??!! I'm usually booked up 3/4 weeks in advance and I prefer a reminder closer to the time as well as the initial invite.

Q. What are your tips for actors when submitting themselves for a role?

As before, read the brief carefully. Be polite and not demanding. If I've seen you in a production then remind me as I'll more than likely have notes on you in my database.

Q. What would be your best advice for actors during the audition process?

Dress correctly. If it's an audition for a rock musical, then use your common sense. I don't mean fancy dress, but a hint of the bohemian would set you up well with the panel.

Remember that as soon as you walk into the room you're being watched, and while you're waiting and getting ready that people are listening. There's nothing worse than having a diva in the cast, so be careful of voicing your opinions as you never know who is listening.

Life as an Actor

Q. And after the audition?

I always find it nice when I get a really cheerful tweet saying how much they enjoyed the audition. A lot of the time you will be waiting to hear - this is mostly down to the fact that a casting director can't tell the no's until the production is fully cast in case they need to see people again, or that the creative team are still pondering on who they like.

Many thanks to casting director Benjamin Newsome for taking the time to answer these questions

Auditions

Auditions are a fact of life for actors. They can be incredibly nerve-wracking and stressful, but this section will give you advice and guidance on how to approach the audition process for a greater chance of positive results.

The basics

- You should never have to pay to attend an audition.

- Ask questions and make sure you have all the information you require before you attend. If this information is not forthcoming you may wish to reconsider taking part.

- Do your research. Check company websites, read reviews or get testimonials from other actors. Whilst some details of castings may necessarily need to remain confidential (both project and client names can be withheld for completely legitimate reasons) and other companies may be genuinely new on the scene, you should be able to ascertain from the casting director whether the client is a bonafide company without them necessarily revealing the name.

- Plan your route and leave in plenty of time to allow for unexpected delays. If you've got a specific slot the last thing you want to do is miss it.

- The vast majority of castings will be safe and professional experiences but always trust your instincts. Before attending make sure you have as much information as possible. Have a contact number and address for the audition: most castings will not take place in a hotel room or private residence. If they are, ensure you know who you will be meeting – will there be several people present? Can you take somebody to accompany you? Any legitimate employer, casting director or agent will understand your concerns and do their best to address them.

- If nudity, or partial-nudity, is required as part of the audition it's good practice for this to be made clear in the initial casting notice, or in follow-up communication to you. There should be privacy and a separate changing space provided. If you are asked to do something that makes you uncomfortable, stop. Do not be pressured into a situation you feel is inappropriate.

• The same goes for Health & Safety. If you'll be required to do any form of stage fighting, combat or stunt performance this should have been made clear to you before the audition and appropriate safety precautions should be in place.

The format

Many auditions will ask you to perform from sides. These are excerpts from the production script and could be anything from a few lines to an entire scene. You may be sent these prior to your audition slot so you can do your preparation ahead of time, or you'll be required to do a cold reading in the room. Other audition formats may be improvisation-based, or a mixture of the two.

Sometimes you'll be asked to perform a monologue, in which case it's worth thinking about which piece will showcase your skills and strengths as a performer, and what would be best for the role for which you are auditioning. You can ask a teacher or another actor for advice on what would suit you, and try to find a monologue which has a clear structure with a beginning, middle and end. See lots of new plays to get ideas for fresh and original pieces which the casting director won't have heard hundreds of times. Read lots of scripts – joining a library is a good idea to help save money. If you're stuck for ideas, lots of actors on Casting Call Pro also recommend looking to films, TV shows and novels for inspiration. You could even try writing a piece yourself.

Some actors warn against doing the same monologue for every audition just because it's well-prepared, whereas others advise against constantly learning new pieces because you risk focusing more on the words than your performance. Try to have a few at your disposal that you're comfortable with in case you're asked to take direction during the audition.

'It might be useful to go to the Actors Centre. They sometimes hold seminars to build up an audition portfolio. Nina Finborough's weekly classes are great for audition practise and she will introduce you to pieces she think would suit you. Avoid accents you can't do, but if you have a regional accent it could be good to use it; avoid pieces in translation; always have at least one Shakespeare/classical piece and a serious and comic modern; try to keep within your age range.'

Miranda French

'Picking a piece which has a 'story' or 'journey' is useful. One that has a couple of transitions or twists of mood is great. I've found a few over the years in the works of David Halliwell, Peter Shaffer and Tom Stoppard and have now used the Tom Stoppard piece on a regular basis for many years.'

Andrew McDonald

Typecasting

Typecasting is the name given to the process whereby an actor becomes associated with a specific type of character, making it difficult to branch out and take on new roles. We asked our members what they thought about it, and what you can do to combat it if you find it to be a problem.

'One of the hardest things to figure out as an actor is what others view you as, so typecasting is a great way to inform you of the answer. But don't ever become comfortable as a one-trick pony. It will always minimalise your options. Combat the John Wayne syndrome by taking on some unpaid parts in low-budget films who are desperate for actors, and use those in a showreel to push you for a wider scope of castings. A variety of headshots will also help, and keep a portfolio of diverse looks from any and every production you feature in. Over time you'll create a plethora of different looks.'

Tom Fava

www.tomfava.com

© Caroline Webster

'I don't have a problem with it. It is just a question of getting to know your 'type' and promoting it for all you are worth! We all have certain attributes that are more appropriate to certain roles, and I believe we should consider them as our strengths.'
Faith Hanstater
www.faithhanstater.com

© Nicholas Dawkes

'I think typecasting is inevitable when you're starting out, particularly in film and TV, as people don't know your work. I try and use this to my advantage to build up a body of work on my CV. There are some theatre companies that I've built good relationships with and have worked with more than once, who will take a chance on me and try me in different roles.'
Sarah Finigan

© Carl Proctor

'It didn't harm Jennifer Aniston's career! Your best selling point is who you are – it's not about being typecast, it's about getting work.'
Suzanne Goldberg

© John Clark

'Typecasting is always a problem. The best way to combat this is to improve as an actor. Join improvisation classes, learn new accents to excellent standards, improve your repertoire of acting styles, go to the theatre and over time it will pay off. However, make peace with the fact that a certain amount of typecasting is inevitable. It's potentially lucrative if you know what your 'type' is and market yourself accordingly.'
Angus King

Tips for Audition Success

'*My top audition tip is really simple: remember that they would like to to give you the job. It's great for calming nerves and worries, and just letting you concentrate on giving your best performance!*'
James Canvin
www.jamescanvin.com

'*Do yourself a favour and minimise the stress of the audition situation by arriving at the audition venue at least 30 minutes early. You give yourself a chance to get familiar with your surroundings, breathe in the environment and also give a practical demonstration of your professionalism, reliability and respect to the project you're auditioning for.*'
Ayesha Casely-Hayford
www.ayeshacasely-hayford.com

'*Be brave and make choices. They may not be the 'right' ones, but if you can justify why you chose to do something the way you did, you're at least giving the panel something to work with rather than offering a beige take on the character.*'
Erica Muscat

'*My best advice for an audition other than practise makes perfect is to wear something that stands out and speaks volumes about your personality, but doesn't detract from the character you are portraying. Whether its a hat, a particular pair of shoes or even a flower in your hair the auditioner will always remember the first, the last and the one with hat...*'
Natalie Anson
www.natalieanson.co.uk

Life as an Actor

© Sheila Burnett

'Always have questions to ask the agent or casting director. You're showing them your talent and you should have made bold choices about your character or scene. Oh, and be yourself!'
Cassandra Hodges
www.talesretold.co.uk

© Catherine Shakespeare Lane

'My top audition tip is to not think about yourself as much as possible and really focus your attention on the other person, from your scene partner to the audition panel. After all you're also auditioning them, so you need to find out if you are in simpatico with them or not.'
Offue Okegbe

© David Woodings

'KNOW YOUR STUFF! Research the company, role and production as much as you can. Pre plan answers to questions you think they might ask. The more knowledge you are armed with the more confident you'll be and therefore the more relaxed you'll be. This should help your true fabulous self shine through!'
Mollie Fyfe-Taylor

© Irven Lewis

'A top casting director gave this valuable tip ... don't take lots of bags and coats in with you. Be 'clutter free'!'
Nicola Wright
www.castingcallpro.com/uk/nicola.wright

'My top audition tip is simple, listen to what you have been asked to do and if you don't understand then ask.'
Thomas William Kelso

'My best audition tip for acting auditions is to prepare as much as you can in advance to help allay nerves – look up your route on Google Maps and run through where you have to go, look on Google Streetview so you know what the street and building looks like, research the company, make sure your pieces are absolutely up to scratch, and think through contingency plans. I like to sit down the night before visualising the whole experience and deciding on all of the possible 'worst case scenarios' at each point, working out what I would do if they happened. With this plan in place it doesn't matter what happens because I've already prepared mentally what to do, so it means I'm more relaxed throughout the whole thing. With singing auditions my best tip is to eat fresh pineapple soon before you go in – it is high in bromine and cleanses your vocal chords.'
Kathryn Usher

'I always have a tube of Wine Gums as they help lubricate my throat to help warm up my voice and the chewing calms my nerves. They are also a childhood treat so therefore make auditions more fun.'
Natalie Gray

137

Life as an Actor

© Sheila Burnett

'My top audition tip is to be prepared for anything and to think on your feet. It is easy to get a preconceived idea of what a project will be like and hence how the casting will go. But all too often they will throw a curveball and ask you to do something totally crazy that leaves you not looking your best. I think they are often wanting to see not only how well you work on the script, but also how well you can improvise, think on your feet and be part of the collaborative process.'
Melissa De Mol

© Claire Grogan

'Do your thinking well in advance so when you get there you can just do!'
Joanna Leese

© Kelly Valentine

'If you have long hair always take a hair tie with you. So many directors like to see hair off the face.'
Sally Lawrence
www.outloudproductions.co.uk

© Adrian Carr

'I often find wearing something that suggests the character you are auditioning for works for me. Some people say don't do this and I'm not saying go in costume, but wear something that helps you feel like the character. (e.g. the smarter end of casual for a lawyer, doctor role etc.)'
George Weightman

© Damian McFadden

'*Be as confident as you can when you walk into your audition and develop a photographic memory for names. Try to remember as many people as you can. You never know if you'll ever meet any of your audition panel again and they will be super impressed that they made the same impression on you as you hopefully did on them.*'

Leigh Stevenson
www.leighstevenson.com

© John Clark

'*Auditions are important for an actor, and an actor should treat them as important and prepare accordingly, but it is important to not let them overtake your life. So, build other things into your day when you know you have a big audition, so that you don't feel everything is 'leading' to the audition on the day. I try to schedule coffee with a friend, search for interesting galleries / parks nearby, check out the local* area, so that I know that I have something to go and do after the audition to take my mind off my performance in the audition. One never knows, the audition panel might want to know what I have planned for the rest of the day, and might be interested to see me using my time proactively in this way. And I might also make some interesting character observations to use for a future role! This is what I do, and I find it really helps, especially when travelling to new parts of the country for drama school auditions.*'

Lucynda Wells
@lucyndawells

Coping with Rejection

Being considered for a role, auditioning and then getting bad news is part of life for an actor. Rejection is inevitable. It's a saturated market and Casting Call Pro members say their average success rate is 1 in 10 auditions – and they consider anything higher than this a bonus! Never forget that acting is a business and there are frequently lots of contributing factors involved in any casting decision beyond your performance.

So prepare well and do your best in the audition room – focus on making a good impression as you never know what project the casting director will move on to next – and try not to take it personally if you don't book the job this time. If there's something you can learn from the experience, or from any feedback – do. Otherwise the best cure for the blues is to pick yourself up, apply for more castings, start preparing for the next audition and keep moving forward.

Going to the gym, practising yoga or doing meditation are all great ways of getting back into a positive mindset and keeping yourself in shape. Have lots of hobbies outside acting and – although it can be great to set the world to rights with your actor buddies – it's always good to have a network of friends and contacts outwith the industry to give yourself a break every now and again! Treat yourself to a trip to the theatre, or watch a classic movie – lots of our members say watching a great performance is their favourite way to get fired up again, and remind themselves why they put themselves through it!

© Michael Shelford

'Spend your energy on becoming a better actor – you have control over that. You don't have control over much else, but you're in charge of your preparation, how much you've practiced, how well you learned your part, and how you interview. So work on the things you can control and leave everything else alone.'
Elizabeth Guterbock

© Scott Cadenhead

'A philosophical approach is key I believe. If you get turned down for a job, it's not the right job for you. Keep busy, keep active and keep perspective. Often rejection comes from a whole raft of other issues that have nothing to do with your talent, your personality or even your appearance. You might just have the wrong shoe size.'
Karen Bartke

Applying for Work: a Q&A with Worcester Rep

worcester repertory company

*Catherine
Standerwick and
Fiona McGregor in As
You Like It*

Q: That age-old question: how long should a covering letter be?
Short and to the point. Covering letters are a great way to introduce yourself, but much like meeting in person, if you waffle and digress it's unlikely to give you the desired impact and it may just bore the reader. Make sure the information is relevant to what you applying for and that you get the name of the person you are sending it to right. No one likes their name spelled incorrectly.

Q: Are there common mistakes actors make when applying for jobs?
The one that really makes a difference is sending your application to the right person. If you send it to someone you think is 'more important' etc, you may risk not being seen at all. For example, any CVs/Headshots sent to the Artistic Director's Office at the Worcester Rep will eventually get to the right place, but more often than not your CV will have missed the 1st sift. Most castings are very clear about how to apply and each company is different, but they all have a system that works for them. Trying to get past that system rarely works.

Q: When it comes to headshots, do you like to see an image that relates directly to a role (e.g. geeky, tough guy etc)?
Absolutely! I like to see a variety of headshots from actors but the one that grabs me has got to make me think your right for the part. Once you've caught the attention of whoever is casting, they will then look through other headshots. Always try to have a few online to give the employers a variety.

Q: What do you think is the optimum length and/or format for a showreel? In other words, how long until you stop watching?!
It depends if there is a dedicated casting department or not. With companies where associates or assistants do the casting there is a good chance that it will be only one part of their jobs. They probably won't have time to watch a 10 minute show reel. Anywhere between 2 – 4 minutes would be ideal.

Oliver Brooks, Ben Humphrey, Richard Curnow, Fiona McGregor and Liz Grand in Jack and the Beanstalk

Q: What are your tips for actors when making an application?

Have a realistic outlook on what you're applying for. Far too often we get actors who are just not suitable for the role. We've had castings for 'Young, handsome, and fresh faced actors' where 40 year old men who would do well as Eastenders villains have applied. This doesn't do you any favours and reduces the chance of you getting seen next time.

Q: What would be your best advice for actors during the audition process?

Try not to be too nervous. I know that's easier said than done but it makes such a difference to how you're perceived in the audition itself. Remember, we want you to get the job. We want you to be the person that outshines all the rest. We're on your side.

Q: And after the audition?

Once you have been given the awful 'no' by a company, don't get too despondent. It could be for any number of reasons. It is very rarely down to your ability. We had one instance when casting for As You Like It in 2012 where one actor was the clear choice. However the final auditionee came through the door and was so like the person who was playing his brother he pipped the other actor to the post. It can be that simple. I will just add the actor that was beaten to that role was later offered two more with the rep... it all worked out in the end. An email thanking the company for seeing you and a gentle reminder once a year that you are still in the industry goes a long way with us.

Many thanks to Ben Humphrey, Associate Director at Worcester Rep for taking the time to answer these questions. www.worcester-rep.co.uk

> "An email thanking the company for seeing you and a gentle reminder once a year that you are still in the industry goes a long way with us"

Other Sources of Acting Work

A way to improve your success rate at auditions, and improve your skills as an actor, is to diversify and expand the range of the types of work for which you apply. In addition to acting for stage, screen and radio there are a number of other professional outlets for your acting talents, all of which put you in front of an audience and require you to get into character, perform, improvise and interact.

Two such examples are Theatre In Education, or T.I.E, which refers to professional theatre productions as part of school education, and Actor-based Roleplay in which businesses collaborate with actors to deliver tailored roleplay scenarios designed to help a company achieve its aims.

Theatre In Education

THIS GUIDE WAS KINDLY WRITTEN BY TIM DAWKINS AT QUANTUM THEATRE

Theatre in Education is hard work. Normally you're not just an actor but a stage manager, a lighting technician, a sound technician and quite often a driver too. (Learning to drive greatly increases your employability in T.I.E.) There are a lot of early mornings and there is a lot of staying away. The average day goes something like this:

5:30-6am: Rise yourself from your slumber, get yourself ready and get something to eat. (You'll need it.)

6-8am – Drive to the school if you're the driver, sleep in the van if you're not.

8-9:30am – Arrive at the school, unload the van and set up in the hall, make time for a warm up!

9:30-10:30 – Do the first show. Be brilliant!

10:30-11:00 – Pack everything down and load the van.

11-12:45 – Drive to the next school and have some lunch (You'll need it.)

12:45-1:45 – Arrive at the school, unload the van and set up in the hall.

1:45-2:45 – Do the second show. Be more than brilliant!

2:45-3:15 – Pack everything down and load the van.

3:15-5:15 – Drive back to your digs and pray there's no traffic…

Depending on the company the style of play will differ immensely. You could find yourself doing anything from a hard hitting drama on the dangers of drinking and driving, to dressing up as a bear for the Christmas panto.

Whether you're making children laugh or cry, T.I.E. is a very valuable branch of theatre. It's an exciting way for children to learn without them even realising it and can really reach children who may not excel in the classroom. For many it's their first experience of live performance and you'll see first-hand the impact it has on them. It's very common to find that after the show you have a queue of children all asking for your autograph.

T.I.E. gives young actors the chance to be part of a long running show, whereas they may only have ever done performances lasting a couple of weeks during training. T.I.E is an excellent way get that endurance training as the contracts can last anywhere between 3 weeks to a year. You don't really know a play until you done it a couple of hundred times! And, as you're doing everything yourself, you learn a lot about the production of theatre on a T.I.E. tour.

There are a few downsides though. T.I.E. companies tend to be smaller and poorer and so the wage can range from reasonable to incredibly low. It's rare even to find a company that pays the exceptional minimum of £355.50 p/w.

It's always worthwhile to make sure you understand the contract. Unlike Quantum some companies will not offer things like sick pay. So if you don't work you don't get paid. Sometimes you'll be paid on a per show basis, so if the company has failed to get the booking you don't get paid.

Life as an Actor

If you're willing to put in the hard work then you can have an amazing time, meet some amazing people and become an even more amazing actor on a T.I.E. tour!

TIE Touring Reflections:

'Touring in TIE makes you consider your audience a lot more. The fact that you frequently get such an instant reaction makes it is easy to know if you're communicating the story or facts as clearly as possible and, more, importantly whether your audience is actually engaged with what you're doing.

TIE can be a great place to improve your versatility as a performer as you're very often playing a number of parts within short space of time. You get the chance to use and develop different physicality and accents, some of which might not fall into your usual castability, but which you are then able to call upon in future work.

I also like to think it makes you a much more resourceful and generous performer. There really isn't any room for prima donnas in TIE. You're rarely in the optimum conditions for performing - little preparation time, no crew, you basically just set up and go on - and yet you're still expected to give 100%. You also become more more adaptable. I've worked on shows that have had to be adapted at the last minute to accommodate an understudy with little knowledge of the show and even turned a 3 man show into 2 man show whilst being at the venue.'
Ali Brown

'Not only was I seeing and visiting different areas of the country daily, each performance was, and had to be, entirely different from the last. I loved the challenge of performing to an honest audience of children, who made each show unique as we had to constantly adapt. Setting up and performing in different spaces was also an invaluable lesson and has made me a more versatile and flexible actor. Truthfully, I now take this lesson to all auditions with me as you are never able to predict the atmosphere and setting of a casting. I am now more fearless in my approach to many aspects of being a working actor! Like many jobs you cannot choose who you work with, and T.I.E. is one of the biggest tests of being closely put together with someone all day,

everyday – *this is not only a skill all actors need to learn, but a valuable life lesson in itself!'*
Sam Harrison

'TIE can be the most rewarding work you do as an actor. It constantly tests your skills and if you put the work in, the outcome is some of the best fun you will ever have in a working day. Students would often ask if this was our job, and we would always say, with the biggest grin, 'yes - our job is to act like lunatics and teach you things without you noticing you're learning!"
Michael McDermott

Quantum Theatre for Science was founded in 1988 as a direct response to the lack of educational drama available to schools on the subject of numeracy and science. Over twenty years on, nearly three thousand schools each year see Quantum performances, using them to introduce or re-enforce these topics, making Quantum Britain's foremost science and numeracy-based theatre-in-education company.
www.quantumtheatre.co.uk

Actor-based Role Play During Corporate Training Management & Leadership Development Programmes

THIS GUIDE WAS KINDLY WRITTEN BY KASSAM JAFFER AT LONGCORD TRAINING AND CONSULTING

In the current economic climate, where upping capability and reducing costs is not up for debate, there is a real onus on those in leadership and line managerial roles to focus their time and effort on the performance management of their team members. On one hand this means line managers inspiring, engaging, empowering and motivating team members; but it also means being able to tackle performance issues in a fair yet robust way, by having the courage and confidence to engage in difficult conversations with staff – those conversations that many managers would much rather steer clear of altogether.

In many instances, managers usually feel concerned about engaging in such conversations, particularly with more sensitive issues, because of previous negative experiences or the fear of saying something wrong or hurtful. Delivering messages in an open, honest, direct and respectful way, while this may sound simple in theory, is a whole different ball game altogether in practice. Indeed many managers struggle when faced with the prospect of a conversation following direct reports on, for example, underperformance issues, inappropriate conduct or other sensitive matters such a personal hygiene, religious beliefs, sick absence etc.

It is of paramount importance for anyone in a leadership or line management role to learn to engage in these conversations, as doing so builds relationships and develops successful teams. Not doing so means that there will be misunderstandings, agreements never reached, feelings never expressed – all because people either avoid engaging in meaningful face to face dialogue or fail to communicate effectively with each other.

A very powerful method of assisting such learning is through actor-based roleplay.

As an independent Human Resource Development (HRD) Consultant running my own consultancy I have been working with actors in training since 2003 and have witnessed firsthand how actor-based roleplay can be both an enjoyable and effective method of managerial training. While there may well be some nerves or scepticism at the start, in my experience managers who are in the 'hot seat' usually forget after a while that they are even in a roleplay activity. This is because, with the actor taking on the role of the employee, it is possible to re-create a realistic situation. This then allows managers to practise engaging in difficult conversation conversations in an open, honest, compassionate, sensitive and assertive way, and in a 'safe environment'. It also helps to improve self-awareness, providing an opportunity for individuals to learn about themselves, their own prejudices, assumptions and ways of seeing the world.

There are plenty of opportunities to stop or replay the action as appropriate, and comprehensive feedback and reflection follows each roleplay which gives the learners the opportunity to make sense of what they have experienced.

When I am sourcing actors for an assignment, the criteria I recruit against includes the ability to play different characters, employ a variety of accents, improvise and drop as many interpersonal clangers into the conversation in order to really 'test' and 'stretch' the managers. However, another important requirement, and something in my view that differentiates corporate training roleplay acting from other forms of acting, is the actor's ability to give good quality, constructive and specific feedback to the manager. This really is a specific skill in itself,

"Helping learners to make sense of what they have experienced in a role play situation is vital"

and not one that all actors can deliver, but it's a key aspect of roleplay. When I find actors with strong skills in both these areas I continue to re-engage them on a regular basis.

Rates for corporate roleplay vary from assignment to assignment and travel expenses are paid additionally. If there is an overnight residential requirement, then all flights, accommodation and food are paid for over and above the daily rate.

There is a lot of work in the corporate training role play arena and I'm always looking for actors who feel they satisfy the criteria outlined above to make contact with me.

Longcord are experts in helping organisations form and develop their talent management strategy and processes. ***www.longcord.co.uk***

Life on Tour

THIS GUIDE WAS KINDLY WRITTEN BY PHIL BARLEY, ACTOR AND FOUNDER OF THEATREDIGSBOOKER.COM

My first tour was as an understudy Dean Martin in The Rat Pack but I wasn't supposed to be on tour. As far as I was aware, I was going to be 'in town' at The Strand (now The Novello) for at least 6 months. Instead, because of some ambiguous wording in my contract, I was shipped out on tour for 9 months. I was relatively old for a first tour at the ripe old age of 28 and I had the luxury of having my own car but still, nothing could quite prepare me for what touring life would be like. Now, after seven years of touring, here are my top 10 tips for the touring theatre company member – the things I wish someone had told me before I started.

1. Give yourself a project.
Learn a new song/monologue, practice the guitar, learn a language. Once the excitement of rehearsals and opening night are over, try to find something that you can show for your time on tour. It wasn't until I had been on the road for three years that I realised that I had just been touring and had no new skills or knowledge. On my last nine month tour I made myself practice the guitar every day and by the end I could play songs I never thought I would be able to. Imagine if I'd started practicing on my first tour ...

2. Join a nationwide gym.
Even if you aren't a fan of gyms, if you can get a decent deal with a nationwide gym or make arrangements in each town to join for a week or so you might find that the nice showers, a swim and a steam can really give you that all important feel-good factor. Plus it can keep you in shape with all that 'road food'.

3. Don't share accommodation with too many people.
During rehearsals, it can seem like a great idea to book all your accommodation to stay with your new best friends but remember, most

153

tours consist of eight shows a week and can last for months or even a year. Book the first few weeks if you like but then try to give yourself space. Book that single room in a lovely family house and enjoy the change of scenery.

4. Take lots of photos.
Time goes by so quickly and you will forget where you have been. Keep a diary note of where you are on what dates and take photos along the way.

5. Save some money.
Especially if this is your first job since college. A good friend of mine graduated from RADA and went straight into a nice job in town. Of course once the HMRC see that you are earning money, where you would normally have a tax bill of say £5000, because you are paying on account for the next tax year, they assume you'll earn the same and ask for £2500 upfront for then too. So suddenly you are hit with a £7500 tax bill and you will be wondering why no one told you about this when you were buying your 5th round for 20 new touring buddies... You never know when your next job might be so make a commitment to save 50% each week. You'll thank me later.

6. Be nice to the crew.
I have been on stage during a soundcheck on the first day in a new venue and seen members of the company moan to a crew member that their water bottle hadn't been rinsed out and another saying how tired they are. On some tours, the crew never stop working. Their 'load-out' will often last into the early hours of Sunday morning, then they travel to the next venue for some much needed sleep before starting the 'load-in' at 7 (and sometimes earlier) the next day. They will have walked into a bare theatre and fitted an entire set with lights, sound and scenery with hardly a break between them. Your 'tiring' journey from a friend's 21st birthday celebration in Soho that you were able to go to because you had the day off, is probably the last thing they want to hear about.

"Whatever you do – be it sing, dance, act, tumble, play, manage or be technical – keep your repertoire up"

7. Book good accommodation.

Every time I got a tour I would search the net for an easy solution and never found one. Instead, like every other touring professional at the time, I would receive the set of digs lists from the company manager for each city we were visiting. They were invariably out-of-date, in no order, had sparse details and choosing digs was a lottery. Company members would compare notes during the soundcheck about how bad their digs were – IF they were lucky enough to find any. I started **www.theatredigsbooker.com** to combat this and we quickly became the UK and Ireland's No.1 theatre accommodation finding website. It still doesn't have all the digs on there but we are working on it.

8. Work on your audition material.

As a singer, I found that performing the same show eight times a week for nine months would change my voice and songs that were easy before were somehow much harder to get through by the end of the run. Whatever you do – be it sing, dance, act, tumble, play, manage or be technical – keep your repertoire up because that first audition/interview comes around much quicker than you might imagine.

9. Keep in touch.

The company you tour with as well as the people you meet along the way will be a part of your memories for a long time but make sure you take notes of who they are and their contact details because you never know when you might want to look them up further down the line. I was once at an event and I saw an friend's agent I met on tour. Because I could remember where I met them, I was able to look up their name in my address book before going over to say hi. It's so much easier to note it as you go than try to remember it later (when you're writing your autobiography).

10. Enjoy yourself.

Not since college days has it been so easy to get a fun group of people together. During my last big tour we were a company of 60+ and on several occasions, we took over entire pubs and clubs. It's brilliant but here's the top tip: do something unique in each place you visit. Climb that hill or visit that castle. We once hired a minibus in Glasgow and took 14 of us out for a hike to see the lochs followed by an amazing pub lunch. Pubs are pubs and there is nothing worse than coming back from a tour not being able to remember where you have been. Go out and see the places and meet the people then you'll really make some memories you won't forget. Happy Touring!

*Phil Barley is the Founder of TheatreDigsBooker.com – the UK & Ireland's No.1 theatre accommodation finding website. It's quick, easy and FREE to find digs and accommodation through TheatreDigsBooker.com – find out more at **www.theatredigsbooker.com**.*

Making the Move to LA

THIS GUIDE WAS KINDLY WRITTEN BY RICHARD C. BURKE, MANAGING DIRECTOR OF INDUSTRY HOLLYWOOD

It is the dream of many actors to move to Hollywood and make it in the film and TV industry. At some stage in their career, most actors will contemplate moving to LA - determining what it has to offer and deciding whether it would be a good career move.

In fact, over the past decade there has been a massive shift in what the acting industry is demanding and it is important for those in the trade to evolve in order to survive and succeed. With major budgets cuts and less opportunity in the UK, many actors have had to look elsewhere for work. Coincidently, the US market now increasingly looks for British talent to play American roles. US casting breakdowns are ethnically and culturally diverse. Brits are widely recognized for skill, approach, diversity and overall talent.

There has never been a more opportune time to explore career pools outside of the UK.

Below are some tips for planning your trip to LA:

1. Actor traps
Many actors are disappointed to learn that they will not get discovered in LA during the 2-3 months of Pilot Season. First of all, you will need working status in order to be offered a job, or even have the opportunity to audition. It's rare that a production company, unless it's a major studio, will pay for your O1 VISA. Lastly, a cheap immigration is not the best route either to help obtain your working papers. You get what you pay for and sometimes this is nothing.

Life as an Actor

2. Plan of action

DO YOUR RESEARCH! There is plenty of information available on the internet about courses other actors have taken. There are also numerous blogs about the experiences of other actors who took the leap before you. At a minimum, you should find out what it will take for you specifically to qualify for working papers. As you go through this exercise, it will help you ascertain how much work will be involved in obtaining papers, and in choosing a lawyer and VISA Coordinator.

Industry Hollywood can recommend a few VISA Coordinators that specialize in this field. These are coordinators with a high success rate who help to source the sponsorship, the deal memorandum and file the paperwork. Once you understand what it takes to qualify for a VISA, I recommend coming to LA for a coordinated networking week. This is a safe and quick way to get useful information. Industry Hollywood can help guide you through this journey so that you can make an informed decision.

3. Pilot season

This is one of the best times of the year. Thousands of hopefuls come to LA for a chance to be discovered. It currently runs from January to April and many new pilots for the upcoming season are cast during this time. A typical actor could audition 2 to 3 times a day.

Unlike anywhere in the world, US TV shows are the highest paid. Pay ranges for a pilot ranges from $20K to $40K per episode.

4. Episodic season

This is also one of the best times of year, currently running from August to December, in which casting takes places for all TV shows.

Current trends do indicate that both these seasons are merging into one long season throughout the year.

5. Networking

Hollywood is a special market. It is relationship driven. An industry referral and the ability to network effectively are paramount. It is advisable to have your headshot, resume, reel and business cards, otherwise known as your 'package' ready at all times as you can run

"Many LA casting directors and based on my experience, advise on using your American accent from the onset of the audition"

into decision-makers (producers, writers, manager, crew, etc.) when you least expect it.

6. Business of acting

It is vitally important to understand business of acting. It is show business. You are your own salesperson. What sets you apart from the competition? Be humbled in seeking acting coaches to refine your skills and help give you an edge, including perfecting your American accent. Acting coaches can be found by word of mouth and, because of the uniqueness of LA, you can often attend a class for free before making a commitment. Again, you want to do your research and talk with other actors.

7. American roles for British actors

Many LA casting directors advise using your American accent from the onset of the audition. You don't want to give them any reason to not concentrate fully on your performance because they're distracted by your British accent.

8. Labor unions

SAG/AFTRA have recently merged into one. The main objective for any actor is to get SAG/AFTRA approved. Although often difficult, there are ways around this like creating or being part of a web series. Again, do your research.

9. Agents and managers

Know the difference between the two. Agents need to be licensed in California and can only charge 10 percent of your earnings. Their focus is to fund your auditions and negotiate contracts on your behalf.

Managers are there to guide actors and introduce them to agents. They can also assist in finding auditions and help with marketing materials such as headshots, your casting type, career strategies and a good acting class. The commission is between 10 to 15 percent on all work.

Note: There are more managers than agents. You will most likely find a manager faster. You can have both a manager and agent but it is more commission. My philosophy is, the more people you have out there to look for opportunities, the better.

10. Lifestyle in LA

Hollywood is the best place to have your base, especially for the first 12 months. A realistic budget is about $2000 a month, including rent. My advice is to rent a room, which could range about $500 to $700 a month. A studio or 1 to 2 bedroom apartments could be about $900 to $1400 a month. Lastly, I would recommend a mode of reliable transportation. Studios could be miles apart. I also advise obtaining a California driver's permit.

When you finally make the decision to move here, you will find it can be intimidating and frightening. My advice is based on my own experiences from 2005 when I made the move to and it became apparent that I was not the only actor arriving that knew no one or didn't know where to get the best advice. It was extremely difficult at times and I vowed that I would share this with any actor trying to come to LA. As a professional actor with over 15 years experience, I know all the trials and tribulations of what it takes to live the life of a working actor in LA.

Furthermore, although it is a tough town in which to survive and succeed, the opportunities to showcase your talents are endless. It's a

"It's a terrific town to live in and build lasting relationships"

terrific town to live in and build lasting relationships. My first 6 months were the hardest and I had to build strong ties to industry insiders. I created Industry Hollywood as a support network to guide actors who want to work in the US. I devised educational networking weeks to introduce actors to LA and my own contacts. To date, Industry Hollywood has helped over 300 actors worldwide obtain working papers and sponsorships including introducing their US representation.

Finally, if there is one piece I would like for you to remember, remember this, 'life is a journey and I didn't want to ask, what if? Live the dream or someone else will.'

Industry Hollywood offers unique products and services designed to make the journey a lot easier for actors from around the world to pursue a career in the entertainment industry in Los Angeles. From US visa seminars held across the globe to Networking Weeks in Los Angeles, Industry Hollywood provides actors and other entertainers learning & networking opportunities that are unique, personal and value for money. www.industryhollywood.com

Moving to Los Angeles: An Actor's Perspective

THIS GUIDE WAS KINDLY WRITTEN BY IONE BUTLER

Moving to Los Angeles was something I always wanted to do, but for quite a while I was too afraid to do it. I didn't know anyone and knew nothing about the city or how the industry works here. I wasn't signed with a top London agent with a list of contacts they could set me up with. But after speaking with friends who had been to LA, and others who were working and living here, I decided to take the plunge, and in February 2012 I came to Los Angeles for a month. I looked at the trip as a way to decide if LA was for me: I wasn't expecting to 'break America' and book a lead part in a successful new pilot; instead, I took classes, explored the city, and made friends and contacts. I was a tourist and I had fun. In fact, by the end of that short trip I had begun to establish a life for myself: I left with a great network of people I could call friends, I had gotten to know LA, I had obtained a manager, who I met through taking a class, and I had begun talks with lawyers about getting my O1 visa.

When I returned to London in March, I started the visa process. For those who know nothing about it, it can seem daunting, but once you know what's required it's actually quite straightforward.

In a nutshell, to obtain an O1 visa (which is a visa for 'artists of extraordinary ability' such as actors, singers, writers, etc.) you need a sponsor. The sponsor must be an American organisation; for actors you can be sponsored by a manager, agent or production company.

If you are sponsored by a production company you can only work for that company, so it's more beneficial to have an agent or manager as a sponsor. Then you need to compose a case or petition – and gathering the information for the case is what I found most time consuming. To be approved for the O1 visa you need to provide at least three out of the six following things: letters of recommendation from industry professionals, evidence of high earnings, a record of commercial success, evidence of industry recognition, proof of lead or critical roles in distinguished productions, or evidence you've had a lead or critical role for organisations with distinguished reputations. You also need deal memos for the duration of your visa. Once the petition is complete it is sent to two unions for approval, and once the unions approve your case, it is sent to US immigration. I had my answer from immigration within 10 days. The final stage of the process is a meeting at the US Embassy and if you are approved they issue the visa.

I moved to LA in September 2012, six months after first visiting. I spent the first few days getting organised – for example, I had to buy a car and get it registered. Having a car is crucial, as LA is so vast and the public transport system is limited. I also applied for my social security card which is necessary for practically everything as it is evidence that you are legally able to work in America, and is required when you book a job, open a bank account, get a phone contract, apply for your California driver's licence, etc.

Within the first week I had a meeting with my manager to discuss how to move forward. She explained that not being in the actors union (SAG-AFTRA) and not having any American credits would make it difficult to get an agent. She also suggested ways in which I could become SAG-AFTRA eligible, which means you can join the union if you want to. Being eligible makes you more appealing to the networks and allows you to be considered for union projects, while you can also work on non-union projects. In addition, my manager advised me to get some footage for my reel of me speaking with an American accent, as being able do a good American accent is vital. She advised that I start taking classes and attending casting director workshops, and get new 'LA' headshots taken.

Five months in and I love life in Los Angeles. For one thing, the weather is incredible; waking up every day with the sun shining is something I've never experienced, being from London. I am always out at the beach, hiking in Griffith Park or Runyon Canyon, and meeting people for coffee. In general I feel more positive about my career and future. I also find that people are more open in LA. People I barely know are willing to meet with me to talk about their experiences and offer advice, and many have helped me find work, classes and representation. Networking is something I didn't do in England, but I strive to do it now.

In fact, I used to be terrified of networking, but I have realised it's not about walking into a room, trying to find the most important person and striking up conversation. For me it's about constantly meeting with new people, friends of friends and acquaintances, getting to know them and asking for advice. You are literally building a network of people, and I've established some great relationships this way. One friend in particular, Robert, went home after meeting me for coffee, saw my showreel and forwarded it straight to his agent with a glowing reference – which is how I got my agent. Robert is my mum's old boss's cousin. I met with him for a chat when I first arrived and he is like a mentor to me now; I'm so grateful to have him as a friend. LA is about who you know, so be open to meeting everyone and strive to make contacts – but of course be safe and sensible, as there are some people who are out to take advantage.

With regards to work, most of the jobs I've had I have found myself on casting websites like Actors Access, LA Casting and Now Casting. A lot of actors here take casting director workshops, and my agent and manager both advised me to do this. In a way you are paying to audition, but if you are good many casting directors will call you in – a lot of my friends have booked work this way. I also take classes that have a showcase or an industry day once a week or once a month, and this helps me get seen by directors, producers and casting directors on a regular basis.

In Los Angeles you have to be 100 times more proactive than in London. Networking, socialising, taking classes, writing to people, following up and applying for jobs are my daily activities, but it is fun and I get results.

For me, there are no downsides to living here. I miss my friends and family, but with Skype, FaceTime and free calls to the UK on my mobile I am always in contact with them, and there is never a shortage of people wanting to come and visit me in LA. I might take a trip home around May/June after pilot season, when things die down for a couple months, but I am in no rush to go back to England.

My advice to anyone thinking of coming to LA is just do it. Whatever your path as an actor, LA can offer you things that no other place in the world can. While it is up to you to make things happen, the opportunities, networks and support are here in abundance, ready to be tapped into. I took a leap of faith coming here, and I haven't looked back.

*Ione provides Skype consultations to actors and industry professionals thinking of moving to Los Angeles. Her 1-to-1 sessions provide valuable, affordable advice that are specifically tailored to her clients individual needs and situation. She has already had success with clients securing agent and manager meetings in LA and others who have begun the O1 visa process. To book a consultation and for more information visit **www.ionebutler.co.uk** or follow her on twitter **@ionebutler***

Access all Areas: Industry Tips for Learning Disabled Actors

© Ollie Harrop

THIS GUIDE WAS KINDLY WRITTEN BY DAYO KOLEOSHO AND ACCESS ALL AREAS

Dayo Koleosho is an actor who also happens to have a learning disability. Dayo has worked very hard to train himself in performance skills and has been successful in getting paid work too, on BBC programmes such as Holby City and Doctors and as an aerial performer in the Paralympic Opening Ceremony. Here he is joined by Nick Llewellyn, director of east London learning disability theatre company, Access all Areas along with casting director, Sarah Hughes to discuss how you might get ahead in this industry.

Training

There are not many places where people with a learning disability can get trained in performance skills. At Access all Areas, we are just beginning a new part time one year diploma course in Performance Making in collaboration with the Central Connects department of the Royal Central School of Speech and Drama in north London. This will be a very exciting opportunity for actors who have not had much opportunity to further their skills. **www.cssd.ac.uk**

I started to learn my skills through my brilliant drama teacher at school and then joined Access all Areas' community theatre company. **www.access-all-areas-uk.org** You need to join a community theatre company to hone your skills – such companies include Lawnmowers in Newcastle, Mind the Gap in Bradford, Dark Horse in Huddersfield, Heart N Soul, Spare Tyre, Act Too, Face Front and Access all Areas in London, Hijinx in Cardiff, Carousel in Brighton, Open Theatre in Birmingham and Lung Ha in Edinburgh. You can find others at **www.disabilityartsonline.co.uk**

Acting Work

As jobs for actors with learning disabilities do not come up all the time, it is difficult having an agent. Access all Areas have the Triple 'A'gency but there is still a lot of work to do to break down assumptions of what learning disabled actors can do. You don't always need an agent as sometimes casting directors will get in contact with the companies listed above. Professional theatre companies for adults with learning disabilities also employ actors on their touring theatre shows.

If you are taking your acting work seriously, then you must get a CV together which has all your contact details on, your education and any acting jobs you have had. You will also need a good headshot of yourself.

Photographs

These days photos can be black and white or in colour. They don't need to be done by a professional photographer but they should look quite smart and not look as if they were taken on holiday or in your back garden. Your main photo should be just of your face, try not to have the sun in your eyes or lots of shadows on your face, don't look TOO serious and definitely not grumpy, but also don't look as if you are laughing at the funniest joke in the world! Try to wear something quite plain like a t-shirt, and not too much jewellery or make-up, though you might want to be wearing a bit of make up if you usually do. The best photos look exactly like you do when you come into the audition room as that helps us to remember you- so take several shots and ask the people who know you which they think are the best ones, as sometimes it is hard to make that choice yourself!

Auditions

If you do get an audition then try not to be too nervous and try and stay calm and focussed. You will need to read a script as your homework and remember it. Practice it with parents and friends and make sure you show emotion from the script. Remember to do your best, give 110% and be yourself!

You may want to bring someone with you if you need to. They could help you get to where you need to go.

Remember that at an audition it is OK to be nervous because everybody else will be too! Take a deep breath and remind yourself that you are a good actor! Remember that the people in the room all want you to be the person who gets the job so they are looking for all the things you are good at rather than trying to find fault with you. The people holding the audition are usually hoping to find out a bit more about you as a person so try to answer any questions they might ask, even if you are nervous. If there are some similarities between things that have happened to you and what happens to the character in the script, they will probably be interested to hear about that, and they may well ask you about other acting you have done so do talk about that – even if you haven't been paid for acting jobs you have probably done some interesting acting work at school or college.

When you are in the audition, if you have read or acted your scene and feel that there are things you didn't do quite the way you would have liked, do remember that it is OK to ask to do it again. The audition is YOUR time to show how well you could play the part if you do get the job! And also, do remember that if you don't get the job it is not always because you did something wrong so try not to worry about that the next time you have an audition. Perhaps you did very well, but someone else was even better, or perhaps the actor who got the job looked more like the actors who are playing your character's mum or brother and that's why they got cast. Try to enjoy your audition! Nobody there will be wanting you to be having a bad time – auditions can be fun!

The job

If you get a job acting on TV then you may be filming on a set. Ask for a tour of the set so you know where you are going. There will be a lot of people watching you who work on the set and many cameras too. Try not to get too distracted and remember you got the job because you are right for the part!

Enjoy the experience as you might not get another job for a while. Hopefully the time will come when it is right again.

Payment

If you are an adult with a learning disability and you don't work or you do part time, then you are probably on some kind of benefits. If you are on disability living allowance then you can still keep that and get paid as an actor. But if you get income support or employment support allowance then you may be able to keep your benefits if you earn under £90 per week via permitted earnings. Please ask your disability employment adviser at the job centre for more information.

The government has another scheme called Access to Work so if you do need extra support, then you can get money to pay for a support worker, taxis or any support needs you may have. **www.gov.uk/access-to-work**. But often TV companies will also have money to pay for a chaperone if you need one which could be your friend or family member if you wish.

It's a tough business but lots of fun if you are prepared to put in the hard work. Good luck!

Access All Areas is a registered charity that manage and showcase innovative theatre projects for adults with learning disabilities in Hackney and offer opportunities for all our members to change and grow through the arts.
www.access-all-areas-uk.org

Finance & Accounting

As an actor you're running a business. The focus of that business will naturally be your art, but there will also be inevitable background admin to be done alongside performances and auditions, particularly with regard to your finances. With acting it's not just a case of doing the job and banking the money – you still have to pay tax. If your tax is deducted at source before you get the money you're PAYE, but work where this isn't the case is likely to be regarded as self-employment – which involves a completing a self-assessment form to calculate how much tax you need to pay. HMRC have a useful guide on this matter as a starting point: **www.hmrc.gov.uk/employment-status/index.htm**

It's always worth contacting HMRC directly if you're at all unsure, or have any questions about any element of tax – their advisors are extremely helpful and nothing at all like the dreaded 'taxman' of old – and there's a wealth of information on their website **www.hmrc.gov.uk**. There's no denying, however, that all of this can get very confusing. There's a simple solution: go and see an accountant!

If you're self-employed you'll need to keep a meticulous record of your work and income – this means invoices, payslips, cheques and receipts for anything work-related. In terms of the latter, promotional items such as photographs and showreels ought to be tax deductible as expenses – but don't take our word for it, however: get an accountant. Accountants are experts at expenses and will almost always think of things that wouldn't occur to you however much you might read up on the subject.

As a general rule, using the services of an accountant will pay for itself: having your tax return prepared will probably cost in the region of £300 but they can usually save you that and more on tax deductible expenses. Many accountants will invite you for a free consultation to initially discuss your affairs, and you can take it from there.

Tax and Accountancy Advice

TWDaccountants
...affordable expertise

THIS GUIDE WAS KINDLY WRITTEN BY TWD ACCOUNTANTS

Below are the most common questions we have been asked regarding tax and accountancy:

'I have just become a self-employed actor – what expenses can I claim against my tax?'

There are many expenses that can be claimed against self-employed income. Everyone runs their business in a different way and they will usually incur some expenditure that is particular to them. By law you can only claim expenses that are incurred Wholly and Exclusively for business purposes. So items that are exclusively related to your self-employment should be allowed eg advertising, accountancy fees, agent fees/commission etc

However many expenses may have a 'duality of purpose,' ie, they will have a business and a personal element and as a general rule you can only claim the business proportion of such items providing you can ascertain a business element.

The following list is not exhaustive but gives an indication of the general expenses that may be claimed by an actor depending on the individual circumstances of the claim:
• Agent / Manager fees and commission
• Travel & subsistence on tour if supporting a permanent home
• Costume & Props
• Laundry & cleaning of costume & props
• Travelling expenses attending interviews and auditions
• Postage & stationery
• Computer consumables
• Bank charges on a business account
• Telephone/mobile phone charges

- Accountancy charges
- Equity subscriptions
- Advertising eg Casting Call Pro and agency books
- Theatre and cinema tickets relevant to your self-employment

If you have expenses that are not on this list you may still be able to claim them. Keep a full record of ALL expenses and discuss them with your accountant. They may be tax deductible.

'I have recently had cosmetic surgery – can I include these costs in my accounts?'

Unfortunately, the answer is probably not. Only in exceptional circumstances will non health related operations to change personal appearance by reversing or masking the ageing process not have a private purpose.

If the purpose to change your appearance was to gratify a private wish to improve or change your appearance then no deduction will be due. However, some performers are able to show that expenditure has been incurred solely for professional purposes.

One example is a radio performer who started to do TV work. She is advised that her irregular teeth are holding back her TV work so she has cosmetic dentistry to correct this. It was established with HM Revenue & Customs (HMRC) that as she was previously satisfied with her appearance then the sole reason for the dentistry was to gain further TV work and HMRC allowed the cost.

'I am worried that my bookkeeping records would not stand up to a tax investigation - what records should I be keeping?'

You should keep comprehensive records with supporting receipts. Anyone who has undergone an investigation will know that HMRC can spend months looking through your records, asking probing questions and wanting what might seem to be meaningless information about your business affairs. This can be time consuming, stressful and very expensive – not just in terms of tax but in terms of your own lost time spent dealing with any investigation.

Prevention is of course better than cure. One recommendation is to have a separate business bank account. If a credit card is preferable, then again, separating business and personal transactions into two separate cards could be helpful. Separating your business and personal life will not only help your accountant but it will also help in the event of an HMRC investigation.

There are three general forms of transaction to record:
• Bank transactions, including payments from and deposits into the bank.
• Cash payments and receipts
• Credit card payments

When deciding on how to record these transactions provision should be made to identify which receipts / payments are cash, bank or credit card. For cash receipts, it is important to identify any cash not deposited in the bank but used for sundry cash expenses or general living expenses.

Personal drawings from the business should also be easily identified. One area HMRC looks at is funding of personal expenses. If you have separate business and private accounts, either make transfers between accounts or write yourself a cheque from the business account.

Mileage records are also important. Even if you use your car almost exclusively for business some form of record should be kept to validate this. HMRC are keen to challenge business mileage where records are not complete.

Given that a proportion of your mileage will be personal related, one method is to record your car's total mileage at the start of your accounting year and only record your private journeys made during the year. At the end of the accounting year, work out the total mileage and deduct the private mileage. The difference is your business miles.

If you do not have sufficient evidence to support your business expenses then an investigation can mean an increased tax bill. HMRC may also make similar adjustments to the previous year's tax bills, add on interest charges and impose penalties.

Please also bear in mind that bookkeeping records and supporting receipts should be retained for 5 years after the HMRC online tax return filing date of 31 January.

'I have just bought some new clothes for work – can I put this cost through my accounts?'

Possibly. The general rule for clothing is that a self employed person cannot claim a deduction for the cost of clothing which forms part of an 'everyday' wardrobe. However, the cost of clothing that is required to be purchased specifically for a film, stage or TV performance is allowable. This clothing is not regarded as 'everyday' wardrobe, it is a 'costume' used in a performance.

The cost of costume and grooming such as hair and makeup incurred by a performer making personal appearances, the sole purpose of which is to promote their business activities, is also allowable.

'Do I need to keep good bookkeeping records?'

HMRC are now able to arrange a visit to look at the business records you are keeping in order to ensure they are adequate for your business and provide enough information to complete your tax returns accurately. The legislation allows HMRC to impose a specific penalty of up to £3,000 for any failure to maintain and keep sufficient records to support a claim made on your tax return

With over 30 years experience in practice, TWD Accountants – www.twdaccounts.co.uk/ccp – is one of the UK's leading low cost, fixed fee tax accountancy services. TWD provide advice and guidelines to help actors and sole traders find their way through the UK tax maze.

Part-Time Work & Making Ends Meet

Part-time and temporary work can be a godsend in the acting profession. Not only does it help pay the rent, it offers greater flexibility than a full-time or permanent job when it comes to attending auditions and castings. Being careful with money and learning to budget can be useful when it comes to keeping yourself in the black, but there can be times when your outgoings are greater than your incomings – so it's good to have a few back-up options at your fingertips to help support yourself.

The old clichés of bar work and waiting tables are certainly possibilities to bring in some extra cash – and evening and weekends are a much less popular time for auditions – but there are lots of different sources of work out there so why not try and find something that works for you?

© Brandon Bishop

'Get a skill that you can sell.'
John Sears

© Michael Pollard

'Try anything! You never know what it may lead to. I found a new skill I never knew I had by volunteering and now I make money from it to support me when resting.'
Lara Bradban
www.larabradban.com

'*I was lucky and set up a photography business, which is now also a film making business, so I was able to stay creative when not acting. For me I would say finding something which interests you is important.*'
Matt Jamie

Investing in an additional qualification can be really useful, or think about the skills you already have and work out how to monetise them. Examples of these could be:

• TEFL certifications

• fitness instructor

• personal trainer

• drama teacher

• exam tutor

• swimming instructor

• teaching assistant

• photography

• translating

• child-minding

• proofreading

• graphic design

• singing and dancing lessons

• invigilator work during exams at colleges schools and universities

• front of house work in local theatres

• dog-walking

• regular singing, dancing or stand-up gigs

• … we've even heard of actors working as football referees or open-bus tour guides!

If it's physical work that helps keep you active and in good shape, all the better.

Life as an Actor

© Nick James

'Working in sales is pretty rewarding: it gets you talking to a wide range of people about their experiences, which you can use in your acting career.'
Miranda Shrapnell
www.mirandashrapnell.co.uk

© Mug Photography

'I work in sales at the moment on a commission basis. It is hard work but as a self employed person I can take whatever time I need off for an audition for example. I can make a lot of money that helps me train more and work on things like showreels etc too. Doing something like this also helps me keep my self discipline because I have to work hard to earn any money: if I don't sell I don't get paid. This helps me to keep motivated and not get comfortable in a job and forget to push myself.'
Bella Clairmont

Sales, promotions, office work, catering, mystery shopping and market research can also be great sources of extra income. Promotions and marketing companies are well aware of how well suited the skills of an actor are to their work and actively seek them out for their books. If you want to sign with a recruitment or temping agency be honest about what you do and what you're looking for and good agencies will do their best to accommodate you – your flexibility can be a bonus when trying to arrange urgent cover or last minute requests for extra staff support. Call centre work tends to be very flexible and some companies such as RSVP (**www.rsvp.co.uk**) only hire actors and allow time off for auditions. Do check out local companies and agencies in your local area. Chat to actors based near you and see who they recommend.

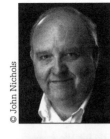

© John Nichols

'Don't just do anything for the sake of it, even though you hate it – try and find something you think you will enjoy, and which could give the added advantage of providing extra income.'
Stephen Aintree

© Andrew Davies

'My approach has been diversity. I've got four or five freelance jobs, on the grounds that if one doesn't need me, another may do.'
Ben Jewell

A-Z of Accountants

BOWKER ORFORD
LONDON
WWW.BOWKERORFORD.COM
Bowker Orford is a team of accountants, specialist tax advisers and business consultants that strive to deliver an innovative service to its clients.We are a long established Chartered Accountants' practice based near Oxford Circus in the heart of London's West End. Our primary strength is offering a prompt and informed service to our clients. Bowker Orford has a long association with the media and entertainment industry and we are delighted to represent so many actors, writers and musicians.

BRECKMAN & COMPANY
LONDON
WWW.BRECKMANANDCOMPANY.CO.UK
Breckman & Company, chartered certified accountants, have specialised in the "Arts and Entertainment Industry" for over 50 years, for both individuals and companies. We are based in the West End of London, near the heart of 'Theatre Land'.

CENTRE STAGE
MANCHESTER
WWW.CENTRESTAGE-ACCOUNTANTS.COM
Centre Stage is a firm of accountants specialising in the entertainment industry. Our services are available, not only to individuals, but also to partnerships and limited companies within the entertainment, media & art industries, whether that be in front of or behind the camera, in the wings, up a ladder or in a studio or office.

GOLDWINS
LONDON
WWW.GOLDWINS.CO.UK
For many years, we have been successfully offering specialist accounting, taxation and financial services to people in the entertainment professions right across the UK.

INDIGO
WEST SUSSEX
WWW.INDIGOTAX.COM
At Indigo we have clients from a wide spectrum of industries. However, we pride ourselves on our knowledge of accountancy in the Music and Entertainment Industry and many of our clients are musicians, performers, producers, writers or are otherwise involved in multimedia business.

MARK CARR & CO
HOVE & LONDON
WWW.MARKCARR.CO.UK
Accountants and tax advisers to the entertainment industry.

MARTIN GREENE
LONDON
WWW.MGR.CO.UK
We are an accounting, tax and business consulting firm. We advise clients across a wide range of industries and are well known as one of the leading specialists in the media, sport and entertainment industries.

SAFFERY CHAMPNESS
LONDON
WWW.SAFFERY.COM

Our specialist team advises both individuals and businesses in the sports, entertainment and media industries. Acting for a wide range of clients, from sportspeople, musicians, actors, directors, writers through to fashion designers, we help our clients to maximise the value of their ideas and free up their time to concentrate on the bigger picture.

SLOANE & CO
LONDON
WWW.SLOANE.CO.UK

Sloane & Co., founded in 1974 by David Sloane, we are a firm of Chartered Certified Accountants and Registered Auditors offering a wide range of Accounting, Taxation, Payroll and Auditing services. The practice is organised on a very personal basis and every client receives the practical help and advice of a senior partner. A wealth of business experience and expertise can be offered with the practice covering all Trades and Professions. All our clients enjoy a personal service, whether they are small or large companies or private individuals working on their own. We also have a dedicated team specialising in the Music, Entertainments and Sports industry, headed up by David Sloane.

TAYLORCOCKS
LONDON
WWW.TAYLORCOCKS.CO.UK

Media and entertainment companies face a unique set of issues specific to their industry. These issues are becoming increasingly complex as traditional media converges with new technology and integrated marketing efforts. Taylorcocks brings media and entertainment industry knowledge and experience to all aspects of accounting, compliance, and taxation issues affecting this sector, providing both a one-stop solution, as well as added value.

TWD ACCOUNTANTS
MANCHESTER
WWW.TWDACCOUNTS.CO.UK

Based in Stockport, near Manchester, we represent the friendly face of tax. Over the last 10 years, we have grown to become one of the UK's leading independent tax and accountancy specialists.

Chapter 5
Putting on Your Own Work

As an actor it can feel like your career is in someone else's hands. A great way of combatting this frustration is to put on your own production. This chapter introduces you to Fringe Theatre, Arts Festivals, funding and includes an A-Z of useful organisations which can take you from page to stage.

Arts Festivals & Fringe Theatre Q&A

Q. What is Fringe Theatre?
Fringe Theatre is independent, non-mainstream theatre. It is often low-budget and less predictable than larger, mainstream productions. Fringe Theatre as a term encompasses both Fringe venues - small theatres, or places that aren't traditionally performance venues but will host performances anyway such as pubs or cafes - and semi-professional theatre companies.

Fringe Festivals are events where a particular town, city, or region will host lots of Fringe theatre performances within a short space of time. Fringe Festivals are notable for allowing any performers (amateur or professional) to apply and with any kind of theatrical content (within reason). This means that performers with varying levels of experience, budgets, and productions are showcased. Usually the only restriction with Fringe Festivals is that the available venues and performance slots are greatly outnumbered by the applicants, so performers have to be refused due to limitations of space and time.

Q. What are Arts Festivals?
Arts Festivals are similar to Fringe Festivals, in that they are usually a series of performances in various venues in a small area. Unlike Fringe, Arts Festivals can have performances belonging to a variety of disciplines - theatre, dance, poetry, visual arts - or may just specialise in one subject, such as the Brighton Early Music Festival.

The level of performers also varies between festivals - some arts festivals will only have famous, high-calibre performers, and a great deal will be expected from each performance. Other smaller festivals may give amateur musicians/theatre companies/comedians the chance to perform, and some solely focus on young people. Some arts festivals can be a great chance for a small theatre company to perform when they're building up experience, but it is necessary to find an appropriate arts festival - appropriate in terms of experience, genre, and budget. An extensive list of arts festivals can be found at **www.artsfestivals.co.uk**.

Q. How does it all work?

When applying to Arts and Fringe Festivals, it's usually necessary to contact the festival organisers and submit an application to perform. However, make sure you check the organiser's website where there will be clear guidelines on the application process - when performing at the Edinburgh Fringe, for example, you apply directly to specific venues. Whoever you're applying to, it's usually worth applying early, as fringe festivals are very popular, and venues can get booked up quite far in advance.

If you want to stage a performance at a fringe theatre, you'll need to decide on a theatre that you want to perform at, contact the theatre, and negotiate booking costs and other considerations with them.

Q. What are the advantages?

Because Fringe Theatre and Arts Festivals are often focused on small scale, non-professional performance, performers have greater scope for unusual, creative performances. They can also potentially attract a much larger audience and media attention than a company might have had back home. A successful performance at a fringe festival has launched the careers of many performers and theatre companies, and can often lead to UK tours or future performance bookings. They're also a great place to network with other like-minded people in a wonderfully creative and exciting environment, and watch productions and shows you otherwise not get a chance to see.

How to Get the Most out of a Fringe Festival

BRIGHTON FRINGE.

THIS GUIDE WAS KINDLY WRITTEN BY BRIGHTON FRINGE LOGO & PHOTOS

Brighton Fringe is the largest arts festival in England and one of the largest fringe festivals in the world. It sets out to stimulate, educate and entertain a wide audience by providing a showcase for all art forms. It is also a completely open access festival, which means anyone can put on an event and be included in the brochure and website listings on payment of a fee. No artistic judgment or selection criteria are imposed on participants, enabling the development of both new and established work to attract fresh audiences, press and promoters.

Taking part in any fringe festival can be a life-changing move. It is important to be clued up and knowledgeable about why you are taking part and how participating in a fringe could lead the way to other experiences. Do your research and find out about the various different services fringe festivals can offer. For example, Brighton Fringe is an organisation that nurtures fringe arts all year round. The organisation connects local artists and organisations to promote their work, to develop professionally and to meet other artists, promoters, venues and businesses. It also works closely with festivals world-wide and international networks (e.g. World Festival Network and World Fringe Alliance) to support fringe productions in their touring, fundraising and professional development.

If you are thinking about taking part in Brighton Fringe or any other fringe festival here are some top tips that will help you make the most of your experience.

So you've got an event, but before approaching venues, ask yourself the obvious – why do I want to take part in a fringe festival? A fringe event is a business opportunity; it can be high risk and a financial return can never be guaranteed. For this reason it is important to set clear, achievable goals and objectives. Think about why you are participating; is it to try out new material? Reach audiences? Make money? Or perhaps you want to get a review before Edinburgh? Chances are that it is a combination of some or all of these things. Before you take part, make sure to plan out every step of your fringe journey – include short and long term goals. Think practically about how you will go about achieving them.

© Paul Kondritz

Be honest with your audiences – do not over-promise or over-egg your event. When putting publicity together, try to think about audiences and their expectations. In all communication it is important to be clear and honest to ticket-buyers. For example, don't advertise your show as being the best time of someone's life, when it may not be. Words are precious in a fringe environment, so be concise and use them wisely.

Use the advice and resources provided by Participant Services. The team at Brighton Fringe work throughout the year to make sure that participation in the festival is accessible. If you have a query or require information that isn't available in the Participant resource-bank online, contact the team by email: **participantservices@brighton-fringe.org**. There are also some great online resources from the folks at Broadway Baby and Fringe Review, these websites have their own participant areas that give advice on marketing, flyering and making up press packs.

Sell yourself silly and take every opportunity to promote your show! Take part in Fringe City (Brighton Fringe's outdoor showcase every Saturday during the festival) and go to the workshops and networking events that take place leading up to and during the festival. As part of your registration fee you will also have access to the Brighton Fringe flyer licence, which will allow you to flyer anywhere in Brighton & Hove (flyering is not permitted in Brighton & Hove without a licence). The Brighton Fringe Arts Industry office also organises networking events during the festival, which are good places to meet bookers, venue programmers and agents.

Think outside the box! Yes, Brighton Fringe is a market place, like any other fringe festival, but this doesn't mean that you can't approach the experience with creativity and imagination. Do what you do best and be inventive! But remember to be realistic about your aims and how you will achieve them.

Hear from past & present Brighton Fringe Participants...
Jessica Cheetham -Spun Glass Theatre, Participant 2012 & 2013:
'Brighton Fringe helped our career in a few crucial ways; securing a great review from Total Theatre, establishing Spun Glass Theatre as a local company and as a springboard to running Scratch Sessions, a monthly performance event in partnership with The Old Market. The

advice that I would give anyone who wants to take part in Brighton Fringe is go for shorter runs and more traditional performance times than you would in Edinburgh as the audiences keep their day jobs! Also, take full advantage of Fringe City every Saturday - it's always packed with people happy to take flyers and hear about your show.'

© Peter Williams

The Girl with the Iron Claws, from Brighton Fringe 2012

Doug Segal – Brighton Fringe Participant 2011, 2012 & 2103:
'Brighton Fringe was the springboard for the career I have now. I took my first show along in

"If you're serious about making a success of your work, you will need to have a long term plan to make the most of it"

2011 with zero expectations and found myself with a hit. The thing I like most about Brighton is the audiences – they are bright, articulate and great fun to perform for.'

Paul Gunn, Brighton Fringe Participant 2012, 2013:
'My advice to others...? Building a performance career is a 'slow burn' as they say. It will not happen overnight and success must be measured in small achievements.'

Brighton Fringe Managing Director Julian Caddy knows a thing or two about surviving a fringe environment. Prior to becoming Brighton Fringe MD he co-founded and co-ran Sweet Entertainments Ltd ('Sweet Venues') with seasons at the Edinburgh Fringe Festival since 2003 and co-productions at the Adelaide, Avignon and Montreal Fringe Festivals since 2006. He programmed and presented more than 700 shows to audiences of over 250,000 people. He shares his thoughts on participating in a fringe below...

'Don't rush in. Approach fringe participation as a business and if you aren't absolutely sure that a fringe is right for you, don't do it. If you're serious about making a success of your work, you will need to have a long term plan to make the most of it. It's probably your hard-earned cash that you are using to bankroll your project so go and experience the environment, visit the venues, speak to as many people as possible before committing. Putting on your work right one year later is infinitely better than jumping in unprepared.

'Once you've decided to take part, set a realistic budget and stick to it. Treat the marketing and promotion just as seriously as the work itself.

191

Putting on Your Own Work

Look for interesting ways to fundraise – anything from raffles, parties, crowdfunding, nepotism, local interest groups, and so on.

'Look carefully to see if there is any funding to be had for what you do. Think laterally. If at all possible, try to avoid reliance on credit. Overall, be totally committed and shameless at all aspects but inspire people rather than be annoying – there is a fine line. Remember that convincing an audience to fund you is a similar job to getting them to come and watch you. Enlist support on your team too, both admin and creative – don't try to do everything yourself, and besides, getting a second opinion is vital.

'And enjoy it! It's a hard slog, so when the going gets tough (and it will), remember it's a well-worn path that you are taking and there is advice to be had from other participants, your venue and the Fringe Office at every step of the way.'

Have you got a show that you would like to include in Brighton Fringe? Contact them in the following ways: Email: **Participantservices@brightonfringe.org** | Phone: **01273 764900** | **www.brightonfringe.org** | **www.twitter.com/brightonfringe**

Arts Funding

Putting on productions costs money. Lots of it. Hiring a performance space, costumes, props, and a cast and crew can be very expensive. Luckily there is arts funding out there to help - particularly if you're doing work that is innovative, groundbreaking, aims to be inclusive to minority groups, or which tackles a topical or social issue. Here's our basic rundown of what organisations can help and the right way to approach a funding application.

Arts Funding Organisations

The Arts Council (which has separate departments for Wales, Scotland, Northern Ireland, and England) is an organisation that gets government funding and money from The National Lottery, and then invests it into art-related projects - dance, theatre, music, art, and many other forms. You can apply for funding at **www.artscouncil.org.uk/funding/apply-for-funding**. Contact details for the Arts Council are provided below.

IdeasTap is a not-for-profit creative funding organisation, that was set up to help fund young people in the arts. They offer funding to arts projects, but also have a very informative section on Arts Funding at **www.ideastap.com/Funding**

The BBC Performing Arts Fund provides financial and other support to individuals and groups who would otherwise not be able to perform. More information can be found at **www.bbc.co.uk/performingartsfund**.

Deborah Williams: Applying to ACE

Applying for public funding can be an intimidating and competitive process, but you won't have much luck if you give up at the first hurdle. Deborah Williams, a Relationship Manager in the London theatre team at Arts Council England, reveals the efforts her team go to support and facilitate creativity, and explains why you should apply.

At Arts Council England we advocate, develop and invest. We have "Achieving great art for everyone" as our 10-year strategic plan and our priorities are around excellence and engagement, enabling artists to create great work and ensuring everyone has access to fantastic artistic experiences. We're also creating things with digital in mind. Digital and the creative economy are areas that are quite new to the Arts Council so we're learning from the sector in some ways.

Essentially, I have two parts to my role. One is to work with National Portfolio Organisations, supporting them and putting together a funding agreement to help them to achieve our joint aims; the other side is working on Grants for the Arts. Here, I am part of panels that make recommendations on what projects to support. I also offer advice to potential applicants who come to us with enquiries. I'm a writer and performer as well and was once in the same position, thinking, "I have no idea what I'm doing, but I want to do this – and I'm going to!"

I don't think enough people aged 18, 19 or 20 submit applications. Get on our radar. Go to networking events and conferences, pick out a list of people from the Arts Council you would like to meet and introduce yourself so that we know who you are and we get an idea of what kind of projects you might be doing. I think it's good for us to be able to respond to what the sector is doing. We encourage conversations to take place to make sure people are heading in the right direction. This means that when applications come in, the knowledge is a shared knowledge and people don't have to try too hard to be seen and heard.

Sit down and take the time to figure the application process out. When you're trying something for the first time, it is going to be daunting. Find all the information you can on our website and if you find you need a little bit more support, you can ask specific questions. We want to make sure that as many people as possible are submitting good applications that best represent what they're trying to do and achieve.

It's great if you've got friends who have a particular kind of experience. Create networks and work with people who are happy to support you. If you are the artist and the focus of the project, then great, but if you can't do the producing or the accounting, find people who can. This will enable you to deliver the work to the standard and the quality that you want to deliver it to.

Top tips:
• Look at the Grants for the Arts web page to familiarise yourself with Arts Council's priorities
• Balance your books. Your income and your expenditure need to be the same.

If you are the artist and the focus of the project, then great, but if you can't do the producing or the accounting, find people who can

- Request feedback if you need it. Deborah admits that her colleagues haven't as much time as they'd like to dedicate to this, but they can offer "a phone call, an email, or possibly a meeting."
- Your project may be great, but applying for Arts Council funding is a competitive process.
- Prepare to think about how you can improve and resubmit your proposal if it is unsuccessful.
- You don't have to come with a finished product. Grants for the Arts is also available for research and development work. The Arts Council acknowledges that creativity takes time to grow.

This article has been reproduced in its entirety with kind permission from author Amelia Forsbrook and IdeasTap. IdeasTap is an arts charity set up to help young, creative people at the start of their careers, you can find out more and join at www.ideastap.com. You can check out Amelia's profile on Ideastap here: **www.ideastap.com/People/ameliaforsbrook**

Other Funding Options

For smaller projects it is also possible to fundraise independently. In recent years, crowd-funding websites such as IndieGoGo, Kickstarter, and RocketHub have become very successful, allowing people to raise money online. Good marketing is essential if essential to fund your production in this way - what makes your work worth investing in? What can you do to encourage people to donate - could you make videos? Reward people for donating? How could you use social media to help spread the word? Making your company and production look as professional as possible will give people the confidence to part with their hard-earned cash.

It's also possible to fundraise in the real world - by holding special events such as concerts and charging for entry. This method of fundraising often depends on your ability to pitch your project to people, and is usually more effective if people are personally approached, rather than being emailed en masse. When raising money independently, it is important to be aware of your fundraising target, and it must be realistic.

Arts Funding: Useful Links and Websites

ARTS COUNCIL ENGLAND
www.artscouncil.org.uk

ARTS COUNCIL OF NORTHERN IRELAND
www.artscouncil-ni.org

ARTS COUNCIL OF WALES
www.artswales.org.uk

SCOTTISH ARTS COUNCIL
www.scottisharts.org.uk

ARTS COUNCIL IRELAND
www.artscouncil.ie

IDEASTAP
www.ideastap.com

BBC PERFORMING ARTS FUND
www.bbc.co.uk/performingartsfund

INSTITUTE OF FUNDRAISING - INTRODUCTION TO FUNDRAISING
www.institute-of-fundraising.org.uk/guidance/about-fundraising

HOW 2 FUNDRAISE
www.how2fundraise.org

INDIEGOGO
www.indiegogo.com

KICKSTARTER
www.kickstarter.com

ROCKETHUB
www.rockethub.com

WE FUND
wefund.com

SPONSUME.COM
www.sponsume.com

WE DID THIS
www.peoplefund.it/arts

SET EXCHANGE
www.set-exchange.co.uk

FREECYCLE
www.uk.freecycle.org

GUMTREE
www.gumtree.com

A-Z of Arts & Fringe Festivals in the UK

This is by no means a fully comprehensive list of the many arts festivals that take place throughout the year in the UK, but it's a good introduction to the wealth of different events that take place each year. Why not check out local listings to see what's happening near to you? It's always worth contacting festivals around six months before they take place if you want to take part.

ABERDEEN INTERNATIONAL YOUTH FESTIVAL

WWW.AIYF.ORG

MONTH: JULY/AUGUST

AIYF began its life as a classical music festival in the 1960s in Switzerland and moved to Aberdeen in 1973, where orchestras and chamber musicians from across Europe gathered to perform and collaborate in a festival environment. Forty years later and the festival has now grown, modernised and includes even more genres of the youth arts movement including dance, theatre, opera and world music. Over the years AIYF has hosted more than 25,000 young people from around the globe, making it one of the biggest and most successful gatherings of youth talent held anywhere in the world. AIYF brings more than 10 days of top class performances from around Scotland and the rest of the world.

ARTSFEST BIRMINGHAM

WWW.ARTSFEST.ORG.UK

MONTH: SEPTEMBER

ArtsFest is one of the biggest, most popular urban festivals within the UK. It is also the UK's biggest FREE arts festival, which means there are no extortionate ticket prices for any of the 600 events that make up the festival each year, because there are no ticket prices at all! This means that you can see ballet to Bhangra, dub poetry to indie rock, without having to spend any money or queue for hours for tickets! What's more, as an urban festival – it comes without the mud! ArtsFest celebrates the West Midland region's astounding wealth of creative talent and shows the West Midland's region as the bustling cultural centre it is. It features performances, workshops, exhibitions, installations, talks and screenings, across the performing, visual and digital arts genres. It provides artists with the chance to showcase and celebrate their work and to raise their profile with the large numbers of visitors the festival attracts. Visitors get to sample everything from traditional to cutting edge arts and entertainment, all free of charge. ArtsFest is a festival for the young and old alike and we really do stick by our motto that there is something at ArtsFest for everybody to enjoy!

199

Putting on Your Own Work

ARUNDEL FESTIVAL FRINGE
WWW.ARUNDELFESTIVAL.CO.UK
MONTH: AUGUST-SEPTEMBER
Established fringe festival run alongside
official Arundel Festival.

ASHBOURNE FESTIVAL
WWW.ASHBOURNEFESTIVAL.ORG
MONTH: JUNE/JULY
Ashbourne Arts and Ashbourne Festival
celebrated their tenth anniversary in 2009.
The company was granted Charitable status
in July 2007 and its primary focus is to
organise a two-week long Festival during
June and July each year. The Festival
continues to grow in stature, now attracting
support from major funders and internationally known performers to this charming rural
area. But not forgetting its community origins,
it continues to provide for the cultural needs
of the town and surrounding area.

BATH FRINGE FESTIVAL
WWW.BATHFRINGE.CO.UK
MONTH: MAY/JUNE
Bath Fringe is a 17-Day festival of all the
artforms we can find (and some that don't
have names yet) in the Beautiful City of Bath,
and with the collaboration of many of its
Beautiful & Talented population. 170-odd
events (some odder than others), performers
from around the world and from next door, in
places from the Spiegeltent, to the secret
rooms of Bath, to the streets and cafés, to
cyberspace and between your ears, and of
course in all the city's best venues...

BEDFRINGE
WWW.BEDFRINGE.CO.UK
MONTH: JULY/AUGUST
Since 2007 Bedfringe has seen over 300 acts
pass through its doors making it one of the
fastest growing performing arts festivals in
the UK. In 2011 Over 165 people performed
in 50 events in 10 venues over 2 weeks. Over
the years Bedfringe has occupied many local
venues turning them into fully functional
performance spaces. These venues include The
Swan Hotel, The Civic Theatre, The Harpur
Suite, The Howard Room and Bedford Gallery.
As well as other more established spaces
including The Bedford Corn Exchange, The
Place Theatre, Bedford Theatre, South Bank
Arts Centre, Esquires and The Ent Shed.

BELFAST FESTIVAL
WWW.BELFASTFESTIVAL.COM
MONTH: OCTOBER
Ireland's largest international arts festival,
with a plethora of theatre and comedy acts.
One of the Festival's key roles is as an
advocate of local work, giving Belfast's arts
practitioners a unique opportunity to present
their work on an international platform.

BEWDLEY FESTIVAL
WWW.BEWDLEYFESTIVAL.ORG.UK
ADMIN@BEWDLEYFESTIVAL.ORG.UK
MONTH: OCTOBER
Festival featuring drama, comedy, music and
visual arts, with a range of fringe events.

BRIGHTON FESTIVAL FRINGE
01273 764 900
WWW.BRIGHTONFESTIVALFRINGE.ORG.UK
MONTH: MAY/JUNE
Brighton Fringe is the largest arts festival in
England and what makes it exceptional is
that it is set in a city with a unique heritage
that has set the pace, diversity, creativity and
innovative thinking in the city and beyond. It
sets out to stimulate, educate and entertain a
wide audience by providing a showcase for
diverse art forms. It is also a completely open
access festival, which means anyone can put
on an event and be included in the brochure

and website listings on payment of a fee. By definition, Brighton Fringe can include any art form.No artistic judgment or selection criteria are imposed on participants, enabling the development of both new and established work to attract fresh audiences, press and promoters.

BROUHAHA INTERNATIONAL STREET FESTIVAL (MERSEYSIDE)

WWW.BROUHAHA.UK.COM

MONTH: AUGUST

Brouhaha International is a professional arts organisation that operates within local and international contexts. Our mission is 'To develop and deliver quality arts projects and programmes that meet the needs of children, young people and adults from a range of diverse communities and neighbourhoods at a local, national and international level'.

BURY ST EDMUNDS FRINGE FESTIVAL

WWW.BURYFRINGE.COM

MONTH: MAY

With an extensive and varied programme spanning a fortnight of events and shows, hosted by numerous venues throughout the town of Bury St Edmunds, there will be something to involve and appeal to every single member of our community. We are an open-access festival and as such are keen to involve as many people and local groups as possible. Whatever your talent, we will aim to find a place for you during the Fringe! We're all about the feel-good factor and intend to place a smile firmly on the faces of all those who live, work, study and socialise in our town.

BUXTON FESTIVAL FRINGE

32 GREEN LANE

BUXTON SK17 9DL

WWW.BUXTONFRINGE.ORG.UK

MONTH: JULY

Buxton Festival Fringe began in 1980 to run concurrently with the world-renowned Buxton Festival, with international opera and high profile literary talks at its core. The Fringe goes from strength to strength each year and now has a respected and professional image with a full colour brochure, reviews of all shows, prize funds and many artists using it as a preview before appearing at Edinburgh Festival Fringe. The Fringe provides a showcase for performers and artists of all kinds in a variety of venues. Dance, drama, music, poetry, comedy, film, exhibitions and magic are just some of the forms that have appeared - we welcome all genres. The Fringe Committee does not undertake any selection, censorship, financing or selective promotion of individual events.

CAMDEN FRINGE

WWW.CAMDENFRINGE.COM

MONTH: JULY/AUGUST

The Camden Fringe was set-up by Zena Barrie and Michelle Flower for It's Alright For Some Ltd, who produced comedy at the Edinburgh Fringe Festival from 2002 - 2006 and started running the Etcetera Theatre in Camden since the beginning of 2004. The first Camden Fringe took place in August 2006 at the Etcetera Theatre and included 57 performances by 22 acts over a 4 week period. It has grown steadily since then. The 2010 Camden Fringe was made of 652 performances in 8 venues. The Camden Fringe aims to give anyone the chance to perform and showcase their talents, from very experienced performers and companies to ambitious newcomers.

CANTERBURY FESTIVAL

WWW.CANTERBURYFESTIVAL.CO.UK

MONTH: OCTOBER/NOVEMBER

The Canterbury Festival is Kent's International Arts Festival, the largest festival of arts and culture in the region, and one of the most important cultural events in the South East. The Festival attracts an audience of nearly 80,000 people of all ages to free and ticketed events, drawn from across Kent, London and the South East. With over two hundred events in two weeks there is something to suit everyone from classical music to contemporary dance, and from comedy to world music with theatre, walks, talks, visual arts, and much more.

ABSOLUT FRINGE

WWW.FRINGEFEST.COM

MONTH: SEPTEMBER

ABSOLUT Fringe is Ireland's largest multi-disciplinary arts festival. Now in its 18th year, the festival stages up to 525 events in over 40 venues, and around 150,000 people have at least one Fringe experience during the Festival. For 16 days the festival transforms Dublin into a 'dream factory', an exposé of great creative talent from around the globe. It is a platform for the best new, emerging Irish arts companies and a showcase for the best contemporary theatre and dance shows touring internationally. For artists, the Fringe facilitates an opportunity to innovate, to cross disciplines and boundaries and to find new ways and places to create work. ABSOLUT Fringe, unlike many Fringes internationally, is a wholly curated festival seeking innovative and daring work that impacts, moves and invigorates its audience.

DUBLIN THEATRE FESTIVAL

WWW.DUBLINTHEATREFESTIVAL.COM

MONTH: SEPTEMBER/OCTOBER

Our policy is to bring the best available international theatre to Dublin and to balance the programme with Irish productions, especially new plays. The Festival is regarded as the oldest established specialist theatre festival in Europe. Unlike Edinburgh, opera, music and dance do not form a major element of the programme.

EDINBURGH FESTIVAL FRINGE

WWW.EDFRINGE.COM

MONTH: AUGUST

The Edinburgh Festival Fringe is the largest arts festival in the world and takes place every August for three weeks in Scotland's capital city. Every year thousands of performers take to a multitude of stages all over Edinburgh to present shows for every taste. From big names in the world of entertainment to unknown artists looking to build their careers, the festival caters for everyone and includes theatre, comedy, dance, physical theatre, musicals, operas, music, exhibitions and events.

GRASSINGTON FESTIVAL OF MUSIC AND ARTS

WWW.GRASSINGTON-FESTIVAL.ORG.UK

MONTH: JUNE

For the last two weeks of June each year, Grassington comes alive in a myriad of colours and creativity as artists, bands, art enthusiasts and local people collaborate to entertain and inspire with unusual and unique live performances, from music, dance and street theatre to workshops, talks, walks and creative challenges. The now nationally renowned festival provides an affordable opportunity for everyone to appreciate the arts in all forms, from classical to comedy. Held in and around this beautiful Yorkshire

Dales village, Grassington Festival also runs a variety of workshops and walks, encouraging people to learn and improve their own skills, and appreciate the stunning surrounding countryside, in addition to enjoying world class entertainment.

HEBDEN BRIDGE ART FESTIVAL
WWW.HBAF.CO.UK
MONTH: JUNE
An annual highlight for the Calder Valley, Hebden bridge Arts Festival brings the best national and international artists and performers to the area each summer for a celebration of comedy, music, dance, drama, literature, and visual arts.

LONDON INTERNATIONAL FESTIVAL OF THEATRE (LIFT)
WWW.LIFTFESTIVAL.COM
Established in 1981 by Rose Fenton and Lucy Neal, LIFT, London International Festival of Theatre, has risen to become one of the most important events in the British arts scene, with an influence that reaches far beyond London. Working with artists from across the world to find new ways of seeing the city, LIFT's rich and varied programming has presented extraordinary events in both conventional theatres and in more unusual spaces such as disused power stations, churches and canal basins. Founded on the conviction that theatre has the power to surprise and stimulate as well as entertain, LIFT has constantly challenged the status quo and continues to actively engage different audiences and communities. LIFT both leads and looks over the ever-changing landscape of contemporary theatre and London itself, offering a panoramic view that will take your breath away.

LLANGOLLEN FRINGE FESTIVAL
WWW.LLANGOLLENFRINGE.CO.UK
MONTH: JULY
From its first year in an impromptu tent on an out-of-town playing field through to its present fixed canolfan Town Hall location, via a converted weavers' shed, the Fringe has increased its reputation with every year. Initially the Fringe's mission statement was "to provide entertainment and education to the community of Llangollen, North Wales". This mission has grown with the festival, and now, in addition to offering inspiring, eclectic and high profile events, we actively promote the concept of sustainability - culturally, socially, economically and environmentally.

MANCHESTER INTERNATIONAL FESTIVAL
WWW.MIF.CO.UK
MONTH: JULY
Manchester International Festival is the world's first festival of original, new work and special events, and takes place biennially in Manchester, UK. The Festival launched in 2007 as an artist-led, commissioning festival presenting new works from across the spectrum of performing arts, visual arts and popular culture.

Putting on Your Own Work

OXFRINGE

WWW.OXFRINGE.COM

MONTH: MAY /JUNE

Oxfringe is not for profit and is run for the prime purpose of promoting upcoming artists who are not yet established and to provide arts entertainment for the benefit of the community of Oxford and for audiences from further afield. Its mission is to provide an open access multi-genre fringe festival for Oxford, including comedy, drama, music of all kinds, literary fringe and mixed genre events, to support new and emerging talent across the arts. Oxfringe organises a small number of headline shows, performer preview opportunities and free community events.

PULSE FRINGE FESTIVAL (IPSWICH)

WWW.PULSEFRINGE.COM

MONTH: MAY/JUNE

Showcasing comedy and drama in the East of England.

SALISBURY INTERNATIONAL ARTS FESTIVAL

WWW.SALISBURYFESTIVAL.CO.UK

MONTH: MAY/JUNE

The Festival blazed into life in July 1973. Since then, over a million people have enjoyed outstanding performances of theatre, dance, film and every kind of music, plus literary events and the visual arts. From mid-May to early June each year, the beautiful historic city of Salisbury is transformed as people flock to the Festival, enjoying both ticketed events and free performances.

STRATFORD ARTS FESTIVAL

WWW.STRATFORDFRINGE.CO.UK

MONTH: MAY/JUNE

Fringe comedy, dance, theatre, poetry, and music in Stratford-upon-Avon.

Audition & Rehearsal Spaces

This lists comprise theatres, community centres and other spaces, usually available to hire on a daily and sometimes hourly basis, though others may be available in your local area. Please check the relevant sites for current information including rates and availability.

CENTRAL LONDON

The Actors Centre
www.actorscentre.co.uk

The American Church in London
www.amchurch.co.uk/Latchcourt.htm

New Diorama
www.newdiorama.com

Jermyn Street Theatre
www.jermynstreettheatre.co.uk

Menier Chocolate Factory
www.menierchocolatefactory.com

Pineapple Dance Studios
www.pineapple.uk.com

Dance Works
www.danceworks.co.uk

Camden People's Theatre
www.cptheatre.co.uk

The Royal Academy of Dramatic Art
www.rada.ac.uk

Chelsea Theatre
www.chelseatheatre.org.uk

October Gallery
www.octobergallery.co.uk

Antenna Studios
www.antennastudios.co.uk

Paines Plough
www.painesplough.com

The New Red Lion Theatre
www.redliontheatres.co.uk/n/n/new-red-lion.htm

Covent Garden Community Centre
www.sevendialsclub.com/room-hire

Dragon Hall
www.dragonhall.org.uk

London Film Museum
www.lfmevents.com

Engine Rooms
www.enginerooms.co.uk

Theatre Delicatessen
www.theatredelicatessen.co.uk

The Casting Suite
www.castingsuite.net

Creative Space
www.churchonthecorner.org.uk/contacts/creativespace/

Acting Suite
www.actingsuite.com

St Martin-in-the-Fields Neville Marriner
Rehearsal Room
www.stmartin-in-the-fields.org/venue-
hire/rehearsal-space/

NORTH LONDON

Big City Studios
www.pineappleagency.com/bigcity.php

Etcetera Theatre
www.etceteratheatre.com

Islington Arts Factory
www.islingtonartsfactory.org

Out of Joint
www.outofjoint.co.uk

Jackson's Lane
www.jacksonslane.org.uk

Bally Studios
www.ballystudios.co.uk

The Factory
www.factoryrehearsalstudios.com

MIC Hotel and Conference Centre
www.micentre.com

NYT Holloway Road
www.nyt.org.uk

Studio 7
www.studio7bookings.com

North London Music Academy Ltd
www.northlondonmusicacademy.com

The New London Performing Arts Centre
www.newlondonperformingartscentre.
vpweb.co.uk

The Poor School
www.thepoorschool.com

The Bridge Theatre Training Company
www.thebridge-ttc.org/b/book-our-space

The Invisible Dot
www.theinvisibledot.com/room-hire

EAST LONDON

3 Mills Studios
www.3mills.com

Toynbee Studios
www.artsadmin.co.uk

The Space
www.space.org.uk

The Rag Factory
www.ragfactory.org.uk

Stage Works Productions
www.stageworksstudios.co.uk

4th Floor Studios
www.fourthfloorstudios.co.uk

East End Studios
www.eastendstudios.co.uk

Apiary Studios
www.apiarystudios.org

The Vyner Studio
www.thevynerstudio.co.uk

Chisenhale Dance Space
www.chisenhaledancespace.co.uk

Number 98
www.ninety8.co.uk

Shoreditch Studio Hire
www.shoreditch-studio-hire.co.uk

Eastbourne House
www.eastbournehousearts.com

WEST LONDON

The Amadeus Centre
www.theamadeus.co.uk

The King's Head, Acton
www.kingsheadacton.com

Soundstage Studios
www.soundstagestudio.com

BBC Studios and Post Production
www.bbcstudiosandpostproduction.com

Jaques Samuel Pianos, London
www.jspianos.com/hire/practice-room-hire

SOUTH LONDON

London Bubble Theatre Company
www.londonbubble.org.uk

Battersea Arts Centre
www.bac.org.uk

Brixton St. Vincent's Community Centre
www.brixtoncommunitybase.org

Arch 468 Brixton
www.arch468.com

Jerwood Space
www.jerwoodspace.co.uk

Watermans
www.watermans.org.uk

London Rehearsal Rooms
www.londonrehearsalrooms.com

St Gabriel's Halls
www.stgabrielshalls.org.uk

The London Theatre
www.thelondontheatre.com

National Opera Studio
www.nationaloperastudio.org.uk

The Tramshed
www.glypt.co.uk

The Last Refuge
www.thelastrefuge.co.uk

Abacus Arts
www.abacus-arts.org.uk

Dance Company Studios
www.dancecompanystudios.co.uk/Hire_about.html

You might also wish to check out
www.rehearsalspacelondon.co.uk,
www.alternativevenues.co.uk/london and
www.cwh.org.uk/tenant-services/
improving-communities/halls-and-
activities for rehearsal space in London.

MIDLANDS

Dance Xchange, Birmingham
www.dancexchange.org.uk

Rogue Play, Birmingham
www.rogueplay.co.uk

RehearseAll, Birmingham
www.rehearseall.co.uk

Putting on Your Own Work

The Blue Orange Theatre, Birmingham
www.blueorangetheatre.co.uk

Stafford Gatehouse Theatre, Stafford
www.staffordgatehousetheatre.co.uk

WALES

Aberystwyth Arts Centre
www.aberystwythartscentre.co.uk

NORTHERN ENGLAND

Hope Street, Liverpool
www.hope-street.org

PHA, Manchester
www.pha-agency.co.uk/castingstudio

Waterside Arts Centre, Manchester
www.watersideartscentre.co.uk

Eurokids and Adults Agency Casting Studios, Cheshire
www.eka-agency.co.uk/casting-studios

The Black Box, Liverpool
www.blackboxmerseyside.co.uk

Upstage Centre, York
www.upstagecentre.org.uk/venue/hire

Britannia Mill, Oldham
www.oldhambusinessandstorageunits.co.uk

The Cotton Factory, Liverpool
www.thecottonfactory.org.uk/tcf/

Chester Music Theatre, Chester
www.chestermusictheatre.com/mainsite

Creative Arts Development Space, Sheffield
www.cads-online.co.uk

EAST ANGLIA

Signals Media, Colchester
www.signals.org.uk

Brentwood Theatre
www.brentwood-theatre.org

SOUTH EAST ENGLAND

Academy of Creative Training, Brighton
www.actbrighton.org/hire.php

Memento Films Studio, Walton on Thames
www.mementofilmproductions.com/Studio_Hire.html

SOUTH WEST ENGLAND

Clevedon Community Centre, Clevedon
www.clevedoncommunitycentre.org.uk

Pavilion Dance, Bournemouth
www.paviliondance.org.uk

BBC Studios and Post Production, Bristol
www.bbcstudiosandpostproduction.com

A-Z of Useful Organisations

ACCESS ALL AREAS
www.access-all-areas-uk.org
Access all Areas is a theatre company for people with learning disabilities based in Hackney, London who run a whole range of exciting and innovative projects.

ACTORS BENEVOLENT FUND
www.actorsbenevolentfund.co.uk
The role of the Actors' Benevolent Fund is to care for actors and theatrical stage managers unable to work because of poor health, an accident or frail old age. Generous support from members of the public and the acting profession itself means the Actors' Benevolent Fund has fulfilled this commitment to actors for over 125 years.

THE ACTORS' CHARITABLE TRUST
www.tactactors.org
We offer financial support, information and advice to actors whose children have special needs, learning disabilities or long-term ill-health, up to the age of 21. We can help with childcare costs and other expenses for actors who are living with cancer or other illness, or facing family crisis.

ACTOR EXPO
www.actorexpo.co.uk
Actor Expo is Britain's largest and longest running organised trade show and networking event for actors in London and Scotland.

AGENTS' ASSOCIATION
www.agents-uk.com
The Entertainment Agents Association Ltd, now trading as The Agents' Association (GB), was established in 1927 to represent and enhance the interests of entertainment agents in the UK who were willing to be bound by a strict code of conduct and professional ethics. Because of its members' dedication to high standards, it has become a most prestigious organisation.

THE ARTS COUNCIL
www.artscouncil.org.uk
Arts Council England champions, develops and invests in artistic and cultural experiences that enrich people's lives. We support a range of activities across the arts, museums and libraries - from theatre to digital art, reading to dance, music to literature, and crafts to collections.

ARTSLINE
www.artsline.org.uk
Artsline is a disabled led Charity established in 1981 to promote access for disabled people to arts and entertainment venues promoting the clear message that access equals inclusion. Initially this was achieved by campaigning with other disability arts organisation.

BECTU
www.bectu.org.uk
BECTU is the independent trade union for those working in broadcasting, film, theatre, entertainment, leisure, interactive media and allied areas.

BRITISH ARTS FESTIVALS ASSOCIATION
www.artsfestivals.co.uk
BAFA is the association for Arts Festivals in the UK, celebrating, developing and strengthening the work of its members.

Putting on Your Own Work

BRITISH FILM INSTITUTE
www.bfi.org.uk
The BFI was founded in 1933. We are a charity governed by a Royal Charter. We combine cultural, creative and industrial roles, bringing together the BFI National Archive and BFI Reuben Library, film distribution, exhibition at BFI Southbank and BFI IMAX, publishing and festivals. We award Lottery funding to film production, distribution, education, audience development and market intelligence and research.

CASTING DIRECTORS GUILD
www.thecdg.co.uk
The Guild is a professional organisation of Casting Directors in the film, television, theatre and commercials communities in the UK and Ireland who have joined together to further their common interests in establishing a recognised standard of professionalism in the industry, enhancing the stature of the profession, providing a free exchange of information and ideas, honouring the achievements of members and standardisation of working practices within the industry.

CREATIVE SKILLSET
www.creativeskillset.org
Creative Skillset is the Creative Industries' Sector Skills Council (SSC) which comprises TV, film, radio, interactive media, animation, computer games, facilities, photo imaging, publishing, advertising and fashion and textiles.

DISABILITY ARTS ONLINE
www.disabilityartsonline.org.uk
Disability Arts Online is a repository of thousands of articles: blogs, news items, reviews, interviews, galleries and creative writing by artists and writers, writing on disability and the arts, which have been published since 2004.

DRAMA UK
www.dramauk.co.uk
Drama UK provides a unique link between the theatre, media and broadcast industries and drama training providers in the UK. We give a united, public voice to this sector; offer help and advice to drama students of all ages; and award a quality kite mark to the very best drama training available.

EQUITY
www.equity.org.uk
Equity is the UK trade union for professional performers and creative practitioners. As a leading industry organisation, Equity is known and respected nationally and internationally for the work we do with, and on behalf of, our members working across all areas of the entertainment industry.

FOURTHWALL MAGAZINE
www.fourthwallmagazine.co.uk
The Fourth Wall – the imaginary "wall" at the front of the stage, through which the audience views the action in the world of the play – an established theatrical convention. Whether we're bursting through it or respecting it, sat in front of it or working behind it, it is one of the fundamental tenets of theatre. Fourthwall Magazine is the fundamental resource for the profession.

IDEASTAP
www.ideastap.com
IdeasTap is an arts charity set up to help young, creative people at the start of their careers. Whether it's funding, jobs, career development, advice or creative collaborators you need, we can help – whatever field you work in. We've partnered with some major arts organisations and we try to bring our members some incredible exclusive opportunities. Did we mention that membership is free?

INDEPENDENT THEATRE COUNCIL (ICT)
www.itc-arts.org
The Independent Theatre Council exists to enable the creation of high quality professional performing arts by supporting, representing and developing the people who manage and produce it. Good art thrives on good management.

NATIONAL YOUTH THEATRE
www.nyt.org.uk
The National Youth Theatre of Great Britain is a world-leading youth arts organisation. We were established in 1956 as the first youth theatre in the world and over the past 56 years we have nurtured the talent of hundreds of thousands of young people.

PERSONAL MANAGERS ASSOCIATION
www.thepma.com
The PMA is a membership organisation for agents who represent actors, writers and directors. It was set up over 60 years ago with the intention of encouraging good practice among agents by encouraging better communication between agents and better communication from agents to the industry.

SURVIVING ACTORS
www.survivingactors.com
Surviving Actors was set up by actors for actors to help and encourage them in all areas of their life as a professional actor. The convention falls into three sections – DEVELOP, SUSTAIN, and CREATE. Events run throughout the year and introduce actors to the various ways of making money outside the profession, using their craft to their advantage, ideas to develop their career; and different opportunities to create work.

THE SOCIETY OF LONDON THEATRE
www.solt.co.uk
Founded in 1908 by Sir Charles Wyndham, Society of London Theatre (SOLT) is the organisation that represents the producers, theatre owners and managers of the major commercial and grant-aided theatres in central London. Today the Society combines its long-standing roles in such areas as industrial relations and legal advice for members with a campaigning role for the industry, together with a wide range of audience-development programmes to promote theatre-going.

THEATREDIGSBOOKER.COM
www.theatredigsbooker.com
Our team of web designers, web developers and customer service experts have quickly made theatredigsbooker.com the No.1 online accommodation resource for the UK's theatre industry. We intend to stay at the top and grow until every theatre professional can find all their touring accommodation here. We think it's a worthy goal.

THEATRICAL MANAGEMENT ASSOCIATION
www.tmauk.org
Established in 1894, the TMA is a leading trade association representing the interests of and providing professional support for the performing arts in the UK. Our members include theatres, multi-purpose venues, arts centres, concert halls, commercial producers, touring theatre, opera and ballet companies, sole traders and suppliers to the performing arts.